THE ART OF FISHING FOR RECORDS

BARRY OSBORN

OSBORN FISHING

OSBORNFISHING.COM

Copyright © 2019 Barry Osborn

All rights reserved. No part of this publication may be reproduced, stored in a retrieval system, or transmitted in any form by any means, electronic, mechanical, photocopy, recording, scanning, or otherwise, without the prior permission of Barry Osborn, except as provided for by USA copyright law.

Direct inquiries to Barry Osborn:
Osborn Fishing
Granbury, Texas
www.osbornfishing.com

ISBN: 978-1-7323728-1-8 | Black and White Edition

Library of Congress Control Number: 2018909855

Cover and interior design by Cindy Garza

Back cover photograph:
Barry Osborn is featured holding the Texas catch and release state record and Fresh Water Fishing Hall of Fame world record black buffalo.

Working with wildlife is extremely rewarding but can involve long days in the field. I would like to thank my family and friends for all the support they have given me over the years. My fishing experiences are some of the most gratifying times of my life. I am forever grateful for my soul mate Karen. After over 39 years of marriage, I still love to unhook her fish.

Barry and Karen Osborn wish you all
the best in your fishing endeavors.

CONTENTS

Introduction 1

Chapter 1 – Overview 5
Lost Records 5
Be Prepared 7
Fishing Location 10
Record Information 12

Chapter 2 – Documentation 15
Collecting Data 15
Paperwork 18
Fish Identification 21
Scales 24
Measurements 31
Photographs 38
Smartphones 43
Witnesses 46

Chapter 3 – Records and Recognition 51
World Records 51
State Records 55
Waterbody Records 61
Weight Records 62
Catch and Release Records 63
Certificates and Trophies 66
Bragging Rights 67

Chapter 4 – Unconventional Methods 71
Rules and Regulations 71
Fishing by Hand 73
Nets 74
Trotlines, Setlines, Juglines 75
Hand Spears and Spearguns 78

Bowfishing 79
Handline Fishing 82
Cane Pole and Tenkara 83
Plnor Fishing 85
Fly Fishing 90

Chapter 5 – Awards and Programs 95
Annual Awards 95
Junior Anglers 96
Tournaments 97
Organizations and Contests 102
Fitness Programs 105
Multi-species Awards 108

Chapter 6 – Secrets to Success 111
Vacant or Open Categories 111
Research and Planning 115
Rule Changes 121
First and Last Light 123
Bait, Lure, Location 126
Urban Fishing 132
Guides 134
Unique Species 140
Multiple Rods 143

Chapter 7 – Mind Games 147
Enjoy Fishing 147
Ethics 151
The Dark Side 154

Chapter 8 – A Final Note 161

Bonus Material – Osborn Overkill Knot 167

Fish Nomenclature 173

Index 179

INTRODUCTION

When fishing records are mentioned people often envision giant billfish, tuna, or sharks hanging from a hoist in an exotic location with fish towering over an angler holding a huge offshore rod and reel. Terms like "world traveler" and "wealthy entrepreneur" come to mind. You do not need an expensive boat or equipment to achieve a record. Many records are obtained while fishing from the shore. There are literally thousands of potential world and state records available in both freshwater and saltwater categories, and you can catch the next world or state record fish.

Writing *The Art of Fishing for Records* is like letting the cat, or in this case the fish, out of the bag. Records are made to be broken. As the number of people trying to break records increases, previous records will fall by the wayside as new winners are crowned. Anglers utilizing the methods detailed throughout this book will acquire the information and secrets needed to replace existing records.

Although I have a Master of Wildlife and Fisheries Science degree, you do not need an advanced degree or special knowledge to achieve fishing records. With basic research and planning, I have obtained over 250 fishing records and awards in different categories including more Texas state records than any angler in history. In addition to my 71 state records, I have acquired 17 world records. My records were achieved utilizing a variety of unconventional fishing methods in addition to the traditional rod and reel fishing technique.

Not all record fish are enormous. This one pound three ounce gulf toadfish caught by Barry Osborn is the International Game Fish Association (IGFA) All-Tackle World Record.

INTRODUCTION | 3

WORLD RECORD
INTERNATIONAL GAME FISH ASSOCIATION

This is to certify that

Barry Osborn

has been awarded a world angling record for a catch
of the heaviest fish of a species in an approved line class category, and that the
catch was made in accordance with international angling rules.

Toadfish, Gulf
Species

.54 Kgs (1 lbs. 3 oz.)
Weight

All-Tackle
Record Category

08-Oct-13
Date of Catch

Corpus Christi Channel, Texas USA
Place of Catch

In witness whereof, the undersigned have affixed their signatures.

Executive Committee Member

President

The thrill of catching the "big one" to secure a place for your name in the record books is exciting, and it is easier than you think to become the next record holder. I will continue to post records, so do not hold it against me if I strive to regain titles lost. Hopefully, we will all have fulfilling days of fishing ahead. Apply the knowledge provided here to find the right place to fish and catch your record.

For fishing guides, the information in this book can be utilized to make money. It always amazes me how the potential of recording records is often ignored by the guiding industry. Several states added new programs including annual awards, big fish awards, elite angler programs, and mastery angler programs. Many of these programs can be achieved by more than one individual at the same time, so you do not have to take away an award from one client to get an award for a different angler. Based on my conversations with anglers some are willing to fork over money to attain their name on a record list. Time is required to learn the record rules, but in the long run, the rewards will be yours. The methods in this book will help you receive record after record along with award recognition.

Regulations vary greatly between states. Ensure you always follow all applicable laws and requirements while striving for records, awards, and recognition. If we learn to protect the resource, fishing can be enjoyed by all for years to come. Master the art of fishing for records and take pleasure in the satisfaction of your record catch!

1

OVERVIEW

- LOST RECORDS -

It was windy, and the seas were high as we approached the bait ball on the north side of the jetty. Smiles abounded from my two friends armed with rods and lures in anticipation of a hook-up from the large fish busting the surface in front of us. My 21-foot tunnel hull boat dropped off plane as the engine was turned off far enough away from the bait ball to avoid spooking the fish. Fortunately, the wind was blowing us in the right direction. Grabbing a Garcia 7000 reel on a 6.5-foot graphite Bass Pro rod loaded with 20-pound test Berkley big game line, the boat approached the bait fleeing across the surface. We reached the bait ball and the call, "Fish on!" was yelled by both my friends as Spanish mackerel grabbed their gold spoons. My long cast caused my Mirrolure Top Dog lure to rattle loudly as it flew past the bait ball. The process of "walking the dog" began as the lure hopped along the surface. The water exploded as a large crevalle jack engulfed the lure. The fight was on!

The initial run took half of the line from the reel as the fish dove down to the bottom of the ocean. The fight wore on, my friends landed their fish, and we began to drift toward the jetty rocks. The battle with my crevalle jack was long and hard with 20-pound line, but the line held up as the process of recovering it progressed. Finally, the fish began to tire. With a large amount of line still out, the engine roared as it started so we could move away from the jetty. It was only a couple of seconds until we were greeted by the loud beep of the engine alarm. There was not any water squirting from the outboard motor, and we later discovered the impeller had disintegrated. Amidst the commotion, the kicker motor was tied down, and it would take several minutes to deploy. We were approaching the rocks so, at the risk of breaking the line, the drag was increased to get the fish to the boat. After pulling hard, the fish began moving.

The crevalle jack was finally coaxed next to the boat. It was the biggest crevalle jack we had ever seen. It was huge! We grabbed the fish by the tail and lifted it into the boat for a quick measurement. The fish was just over 54 inches long with a large girth and easily maxed out my 50-pound scale. Although the fish was much bigger than any crevalle jack we had landed, we were nervous about getting too close to the jetty rocks. To save the magnificent fish, we dropped it over the side and watched it swim away. Fortunately, after untying and lowering the kicker motor, it started immediately as we moved away from the jetty. It was a great day of fishing and spirits were high as we headed back to the harbor.

We loaded the boat on a trailer, bought a new impeller, and spent a few hours replacing the old one. After a long evening, the image of the massive crevalle jack kept coming back to me. Curiosity soon got the best of me, and I looked up the Texas state record for a crevalle jack. The documented record was 52.25 inches and 50.25 pounds set in 1976. The International Game Fish Association (IGFA) line class record was 47 pounds on 20-pound line. Although the crevalle jack did not exceed the all-tackle world record of over 60 pounds, it easily exceeded the line class world record for 20-pound test line. I had landed a line class world record and state record fish without the proper documentation required to record the catch.

There are hundreds of record size fish caught every year throughout the United States, including several potential world and state record fish. The majority of these records are never recorded because most people do not realize there are many record categories and fishing methods that allow a fish to be listed in the record books. It is crazy to think how many fish you have landed over the years that might have been state records, or even world record fish. Some of them may have been multi-category record breakers. In my case, many of my fishing records were not recorded due to a lack of knowledge about the rules. You may be able to recall stories about monster fish you caught and released without a second thought. The tips and secrets in the following chapters will ensure you never have to think "what if" again. The records are there for the taking…all you have to do is learn the art of fishing for records and get fishing!

- BE PREPARED -

The morning was clear, and the waves were low as we moved outside the jetties on the Texas coast. The majestic sunrise and clear blue water brought a smile to my face as the state record length requirements ran through my mind. It was a fantastic morning. Birds were hitting the water near large bait balls of striped anchovies floating across the Gulf of Mexico. The excitement was building as we moved close to a bait ball for a cast. My wife Karen and our good friends Ken and Kim were looking forward to the fishing day ahead. Ken and Kim had been gracious enough to invite us on their boat, and Ken was aware of my desire to set a state record.

As we approached a group of birds, a large bait ball appeared at the water's surface. Below the bait ball, the blue, yellow, and green colors of large and small predatory fish were visible. The depths revealed large numbers of crevalle jack, Spanish mackerel, little tunny, blacktip sharks, and spinner sharks. Ken maneuvered his 24 foot Sea Pro boat into position upwind of the bait ball and began casting a gold spoon. He immediately caught a nice Spanish mackerel.

Suddenly, Kim's rod bent over hard as a crevalle jack stripped line off her reel. She was fishing for Spanish mackerel, and her setup was not ideal for a fish of this size. The fight was challenging on a small rod, and Kim was relieved as the powerful potential record fish began to tire. After nearly half an hour Ken reached over the gunnel and grabbed Kim's 39-inch crevalle jack.

The crevalle jack qualified for a big fish award and was one of the five fish Kim needed for her Texas Parks and Wildlife Department Saltwater Elite Angler Award qualification. It was the first record catch of the trip, but it would not be the last.

The next several hours were amazing as we all boated numerous fish. By the end of the day, each of us landed several potential records including three of my fish that were later confirmed as catch and release state records for crevalle jack, Spanish mackerel, and little tunny on a fly rod. Although I have landed larger fish for each of these species, preparation and data collection was the reason I was able to achieve my goals and set my records.

Always be prepared if you want to set fishing records. Printing the requirements for establishing records is one of the best ways to make sure you do not miss a record catch. Current record information should be printed and kept with you when fishing in case internet access is not available. Instead of relying on your memory printing the record information will allow you to confirm the correct data, potentially preventing a missed record.

Typically you only need basic equipment to document a record. For states with catch and release records, a camera, measuring device, and a witness is usually all that is needed. Weight records take more work and planning to achieve. Most states require fish to be weighed on a certified scale, while others insist fish be taken to a specific location to be weighed on a certified or legal-for-trade scale. Some states require fish to be weighed before they are frozen or within a specific timeframe after a catch is made. Retaining fish after the weighing process may be necessary.

All state fish and wildlife departments, the IGFA, and the Fresh Water Fishing Hall of Fame (FFHF) require completing a submittal form before they will review a record catch. Print this form and become familiar with it before you go fishing. You can make a checklist based on the form so you will remember all the steps needed to document a record. This checklist should be with you at all times when fishing so in the excitement of the moment you do not forget to record critical data about your catch. If you forget a very simple step,

Equipment for documenting fish records often includes paperwork, writing devices, measuring devices, cameras, phones, scales, and a waterproof bag to keep all items dry.

such as taking a picture of yourself with the fish, you will eliminate your potential record. Time spent reviewing record requirements before fishing will pay off after you have landed a record.

- FISHING LOCATION -

Karen, our daughter Cindy and I were anchored beside a channel near Islamorada in the Florida Keys. The boat rocked slightly in the waves as we waited for tarpon to find our bait. Hooking tarpon can be challenging and proper timing when setting the hook is critical. After a thump on her line, it was exciting to see Cindy run to the back of the boat to allow the tarpon time to inhale her bait. The line tightened as the circle hook lodged into the fish's mouth. The fight was on! The fish rocketed out of the water, and its silver scales glimmered in the sunlight. It was a nice tarpon that we estimated to be about 150 pounds. Two more jumps and then the tarpon took off toward the reef. We had already tied a buoy to the anchor line and quickly tossed it over the gunnel as we sped off in hot pursuit of the fish.

After a 45 minute battle, my daughter finally brought the fish to the side of the boat. The tarpon was six feet eight inches long. Since Cindy caught the fish in Florida on a rod and reel, it was not a record. However, if she had caught the same fish in Louisiana on a fly rod, she could have landed a new state record. The location and method you use to catch fish are important in setting records.

There are a variety of ways to achieve fishing records, awards, and recognition. State requirements vary widely concerning fishing recognition programs. Many states have multiple award categories including weight awards, catch and release awards, categories for different fishing methods, annual award programs, and combination species angler award programs with titles such as elite or master angler awards. Other states only have basic species recognition by weight. Because of this, these state records are usually difficult to replace. If you are trying to achieve state records, awards, or recognition, it is easier to do so in a state with a large and varied program. Travel may be the best way to earn a record catch.

Fishing locations containing large individuals of a target species will improve your chances for record fish. Cindy Garza is releasing her tarpon caught in Islamorada, Florida.

Historically some species of fish have been so heavily pursued that you may have to travel to a specific location to catch a record fish. For other species, records may be readily available a few miles from your home. To increase your chances of a record catch, it is always best to fish in an area where big fish of a specific species reside. Checking the existing fish record lists to determine the size of fish in a particular waterbody is a great way to find a good fishing location. Although not always the case, if a waterbody record for a particular fish species is smaller than the record weight or length of fish you are pursuing then that waterbody might not be the best location to land a record catch. Fish and wildlife departments conduct fish surveys in various waterbodies. These surveys can be invaluable resources in determining the most productive waterbody to fish.

The time of year you fish is important. While fishing from a pier in Florida, an angler told me he was trying to catch a cobia. He drove from a northwestern state because he always wanted to catch a big one. He fished all week, but he had not seen a single cobia. I broke the news to him gently, and he was surprised to learn that although you can always catch a stray cobia in Florida any time of the year, typically cobia are not found in the Florida panhandle during the time of year we were fishing. Always check a fish season chart or calendar before choosing a place to fish when pursuing a specific species.

- RECORD INFORMATION -

It was a slow morning of freshwater fly fishing without landing a single fish. My stomach was growling, and thoughts of a hot meal were causing me to think about picking up my gear and heading for the house. Getting "skunked" is undesirable when fishing, and the largemouth bass and common carp were neither biting on the surface nor interested in my sinking fly.

Taking out an elk hair ant fly to catch bluegill seemed like a good way to get something to the shore. Bluegills are plentiful in the lake, so my expectations were high. The fly gently hit the water and settled under a large overhanging buttonbush. A tug on the line triggered a powerful hook set. The fish flew into the air from the force of the rod and returned to the water a few feet in front of me. I stripped in the 4.5-inch fish and examined it carefully. To my surprise, the fish was not a bluegill. Instead, it was a longear sunfish. Reaching into my pocket, the waterbody record list indicated there was not an entry for a longear sunfish. A forty mile trip to the state inland fish hatchery revealed the fish weighed in at a whopping 0.07 pounds, a new waterbody record for the lake.

Many records have been achieved since my longear sunfish, and even though a rule change removed the record from the state's webpage, it is still one of my favorite records since preparation was the key to setting it. Printing off the waterbody record list for the lake and possessing enough knowledge to identify the species is what solidified the record. The 0.07-pound, 4.5-inch longear sunfish, is not the longest or heaviest longear sunfish I have caught. However, it is a catch where knowing the rules resulted in a record.

A state's fish and wildlife website provides record fishing rules, regulations, and guidance. IGFA world record information is located online at igfa.org or can be downloaded from the IGFA application (app). Freshwater FFHF world record information can be obtained by visiting the freshwater-fishing.org website.

Rules continually change so examine record keeping organizations and regulatory websites to avoid missed opportunities and to comply with the law. Record organizations have expanded their recognition programs over the last few years. These programs have greatly added to the possibilities of records that can be gained in multiple categories resulting in a variety of fishing awards.

Sometimes changes in the rules can make it easier to get a record, and other times rule changes can make it more difficult to achieve a record. The longear sunfish mentioned previously would not currently qualify as a Texas record since the Texas Parks and Wildlife Department established a policy that only fish weighing over 0.5 pounds can be recorded as a record unless you are a junior angler. Paying close attention to the rules when you catch a fish will help increase your chances of having your record documented.

The time to achieve a single record is a valuable investment because this initial effort will allow anglers to capitalize on their experiences to acquire further records. Through time and practice, anglers can set additional records for the same fish species, or they can choose to extrapolate their knowledge to achieve records for other fish species. The recognition opportunities are abundant.

The information provided throughout this book will help you acquire several types of fishing records. The extensive details may seem overwhelming at first, but once you digest the information you can master the art of fishing for records.

DOCUMENTATION

- COLLECTING DATA -

Fly fishing from the shore was successful all morning. Several large common carp and a couple of channel catfish ended up in the landing net. The fishing action was starting to slow down when a tail waving in the muddy water a few inches below the surface attracted my attention. The tail was dark and did not appear to be another common carp. The floating fly on my rod was not appropriate for the occasion and the excitement built while running back to my van a few yards away. The goal was to obtain another fly rod rigged with a sinking fly and line. When returning to the water's edge, to my surprise and delight, the feeding fish was still there.

The first cast landed directly beside the fish's tail, and the gleam of the hook faded as the fly sank out of sight. The chances of the fish grabbing the fly were slim, but as the tail turned slightly, the fly line tightened. The excitement started buck fever or in this case fish fever. The hook set resulted in a screaming reel. The first run of the fish was spectacular. It stripped off fly line and went well into the backing as it headed away from the shoreline toward the middle of the reservoir. The fish swam deep, and my enthusiasm sank as the fish became entangled in an underwater rock. After applying light pressure on the fish, it pulled free from the obstacle. My mind drifted to an unsettling thought concerning how much damage had occurred to the leader.

The mule deer hair fly was tied on a small number 2 Mustad UltraPoint hook. By this point in the fight pressure on the fish would either straighten out the hook or break the leader resulting in a lost fish. The fight was long, and by maintaining constant slight tension, the backing, fly line, and leader were slowly worked back onto the reel. The species of the fish was still a mystery as the reel continued to fill. Losing the fish now would be a nightmare since its identity would never be revealed. After approximately half an hour, the fish swam close to the shore. The fish rolled, and it was obvious the fish was a nice sized smallmouth buffalo. The fish would easily result in a lake waterbody record on a fly rod, and it appeared to be long enough to count toward my freshwater elite angler award.

Equipment for documenting records is usually part of my fishing gear, but on this day an unexpected trip to the lake resulted in fishing without the proper equipment. Fortunately, my fishing location was only a couple of minutes from my house, and my lovely wife Karen knows how important fishing records are to me. My cell phone was removed from my pocket as the fight continued. Karen answered, "Do I just need to bring the measuring board and the scales or did you forget the camera too?" I love my wife. She gathered up the camera, scales, and the measuring board then headed for the lake. When she arrived, the fish was close to the shore.

The smallmouth buffalo was a lake record at 30.5 inches in length but one and a half inches short of qualifying for a big fish award toward my freshwater elite angler recognition. The fish maxed out my ten-pound certified scale. A certified scale located 40 miles away could weigh a fish over ten pounds but to use that scale would not allow me to keep the fish alive. Karen called a local butcher shop and asked for a strange favor. We put the fish in a recycle tote filled with water. We loaded the tote into the van and hurried to the shop. After zeroing the certified scale with a big bucket, we placed the fish in the bucket and weighed it. The customers in the store were enthusiastic about weighing the fish because the fish was large and would only fit in the bucket halfway. The smallmouth buffalo weighed 17.4 pounds on the legal-for-trade scale. We threw the fish back in the tote and

DOCUMENTATION | 17

Not every fish caught or partially caught, will be in a condition for obtaining a record. When you catch a potential record fish, make sure you have proper documentation equipment. Laura Osborn is holding what remains of a blue runner that met with a great barracuda.

headed to the lake for a quick release. Water moved over the fish's gills and revived the smallmouth buffalo. We were pleased as we watched the fish swim out of sight. With the help of the butcher, it was a great opportunity to keep the fish alive while achieving a weight record.

You should always remember to have the required documentation equipment readily available to record your record fish. Usually, this means carrying the necessary items to the waterbody where you are fishing. By having the proper equipment available, you can document a weight or length record on a fish you cannot legally take from the waterbody. States differ on how they regulate temporarily holding a fish so make sure you understand the regulations before you retain a fish for measurements, weight, or while taking a picture. If you do not have the required equipment, think about other options before giving up your record. Equipment and witnesses may be available. Yelling, "Hey, could you help me?" has worked in the past.

- PAPERWORK -

It was an exhilarating morning of fishing as Karen caught striped bass, hybrid striped bass, and white bass. We both landed multiple fish including a waterbody record white bass for each of us. Karen was fishing in the back of the boat when she set the hook on a fish. She laughed as she shouted, "Fish on…but it's a little one." After a short fight, she pulled the fish into the boat. It was a small yellow bass. To my dismay, I had the wrong record list for the lake. Yellow bass are small, and this one did not seem like a big specimen. Therefore Karen unhooked the fish and dropped it over the side. When we got back to the hotel room, we pulled up the correct list to check the yellow bass record size for the lake. Surprisingly, we discovered there was a vacant yellow bass category. Another fishing record lost.

Paperwork can be an annoying part of setting records. After a week of fishing at the coast, a few hours were required to finalize multiple record submittal forms for the Texas Parks and Wildlife Department. However, years later, many of those records remain on the books. For us, the time investment was worth the work.

DOCUMENTATION | 19

Although paperwork is arduous, accurate documentation is critical to achieving your record. Pictures like the leader touch on this sailfish are useful when recording a record.

Before you begin fishing, invest time and money in printing and researching all the potential types of records that can be achieved in the area where you will be fishing. Paperwork takes up space, and an additional bag may be required to carry the needed documentation equipment. Usually, paperwork consists of waterbody record lists and state record lists including other method categories and catch and release records. World record lists should be thoroughly read and reviewed including line, tippet, and catch and release world record information. Shuffling through paperwork while trying to fill out submittal forms can be awkward when standing on a jetty with the wind blowing 25 miles per hour, but that is one of the reasons why there are so many fishing records still available.

Official record documentation usually begins at a waterbody by quickly scratching down data on a submittal form. Forms often get wet or bloody so use a draft copy to quickly jot down information to reduce the time required for paperwork during the fishing experience. To record the data, you will need a recording instrument like a pen, pencil, paper, or an electronic recording device. Remember, when you are miles down a river, it is hard to find a pencil if you do not have one. Fishing often occurs in areas where internet service is not available, so it is a good idea to keep a writing tool on hand.

After fishing, and unless a signature is needed, transfer the draft document information onto a clean form within a day or two to prevent the loss of important facts concerning the catch. Fishing record documentation for existing species should be verified on appropriate websites to make a final determination that a fish is a potential record. Organizations that certify records are busy, and there is no reason to submit a fish that slows down the verification process for other anglers if your fish does not qualify as a record. Verification is also important with IGFA records since there is an associated cost involved.

Database searches should be conducted in several categories to keep from missing potential records. Officially recording the required data for a record takes time. Most states and organizations have deadlines to submit a record based on the date the fish was caught. Take care not to let record forms collect dust and never get submitted.

Scan or copy the entire packet of information you will be sending including pictures. Make sure forms are signed and the information you record is accurate. Check phone numbers, email addresses, and witness information. As necessary, make sure forms are notarized. Most record-keeping organizations require a notary for world or state records but may not require a notary for annual records or waterbody records. Assemble your submittal packet well before the deadline in case there are issues during the mailing process or if paperwork is lost. On one occasion, having a copy of my submittal packet saved a record due to lost paperwork at the certifying agency.

- FISH IDENTIFICATION -

Karen and I were fishing from the shore as wind-driven waves began pounding the jetty rocks. After each cast, we kept getting hung on the bottom. Karen indicated she wanted to move back into the bay to fish in a sheltered area to get out of the wind. We decided to move to a backwater channel away from the Intracoastal Waterway. Karen's squid and weight made ripples across the water as they landed on the edge of the channel. While baiting my hook, Karen shouted, "Fish on!" There was not a big run of line off the reel, or a screaming drag, but the fish pulled, and the rod tip jerked as Karen reeled it in. As she lifted the fish from the water, hanging on the hook was an unusual looking specimen. It looked similar to a puffer fish, but it was large and had an interesting pattern.

A quick glance at a book called *Fishes of the Gulf of Mexico* confirmed the fish was a smooth puffer. The record list we printed earlier indicated a vacant record existed for a smooth puffer for the bay where we were fishing. We recorded the weight and length, took a picture of Karen with the fish, and executed a quick release. The smooth puffer was later confirmed as a waterbody record for the bay.

Many records are lost because an angler does not properly identify fish species. I carry books to help identify fish. Several books are available including general identification books as well as scientific books to classify obscure species. Many fish reference books only cover commonly known game fish species found in an area, but it is often obscure little-known species that can provide a record. For these species, a technical book may be required for identification. You do not want to forfeit a record for a black crappie because you identified it as a white crappie, or forfeit a record for an almaco jack because you identified it is a juvenile greater amberjack.

The internet contains websites to help you identify fish species. These can be general or highly technical databases. If you do not know the species of fish caught, finding a picture to determine the fish's general category is usually possible with internet access. However, relying solely on the internet is a mistake. It may take extensive time to find a picture for fish identification. This lost time will take away from precious opportunities catching fish. A book is often a faster reference if you are familiar with the way it is organized. State fish and wildlife representatives can assist with fish identification. On more than one occasion, a university or aquatic research facility has provided species confirmation for my record fish.

Resident anglers are sometimes helpful when identifying fish. Be careful when taking their advice so that a common or local name for a fish does not cause you to misidentify a record. While fishing in Florida on a party boat with 30 other anglers, a white grunt picked up my squid. When the fish hit the deck, the deckhand on the boat hastily walked up to me and identified the species as a white snapper. I indicated the fish was a white grunt and the deckhand looked surprised. He walked closer to me and said, "It is a white grunt, but don't tell the other anglers. We have caught several of them today, and nobody wants to eat a grunt."

Further complications occur when you fish in different areas of the country. For example, if you catch a species locally identified as a croaker, there are more than 20 different species of fish from 16 different genera locally called croaker in the United States alone. The most common croaker species caught on the east coast is the Atlantic croaker while on the west coast it is the white croaker. Both species are usually just called croaker by local anglers. There are also different names for the same fish species in different parts of the country, and

DOCUMENTATION | 23

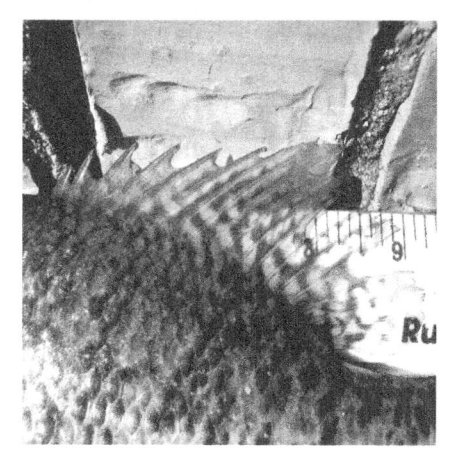

The close-up picture of the dorsal spines on this white crappie helped a biologist identify its species resulting in a waterbody record on a fly rod. Additional correspondence may have been required without providing this picture.

some species have similar common names creating a problem for species identification. If you tell people you caught a dolphin (*Coryphaena hippurus*), many people will think you are talking about the adorable bottlenose dolphin (*Tursiops truncatus*) mammal instead of a large blue, yellow, and green fish. In Hawaii dolphin are called mahi-mahi, but in Mexico, they are often called dorado. Fish identification is not only a problem when submitting information for records, but it can become a legal issue. You may have to explain to a game warden why you retained a protected fish species after the warden provides the proper identification of the fish.

To solve the problem of species identification, the scientific community uses the Latin binomial nomenclature system. This system results in a particular species being assigned one scientific name throughout the world. As a result, each specific fish has a unique recognized scientific genus and species name. The scientific name of a fish is usually listed on the state fish and wildlife department website. In some cases, you may need to contact the record keeping organization to determine the actual species of fish being recorded as a record. All scientific names of fish species referenced in this book are located within the Fish Nomenclature section. This section also contains common and local names for each fish species.

Being able to identify a fish species correctly saves you time by avoiding recording weights and taking measurements on a fish that does not meet the record size or weight requirements. Research information about fish species in the area you will be fishing. Besides providing interesting information, your efforts will assist you in achieving your fishing record goals.

- SCALES -

The cold February wind sent shivers through us. Karen was frustrated with the slow fishing in the bay near Port Aransas, Texas. This was our third trip to the coast trying to catch the last fish she needed to complete her saltwater elite angler award. We had already fished one day without results, and Karen did not land a fish large enough

DOCUMENTATION | 25

Common names vary locally for many fish species. This *Coryphaena hippurus* is often called dolphin, dorado, or mahi-mahi. Barry and Karen Osborn are holding Karen's bull dolphin off the coast near Islamorada, Florida.

to achieve her recognition. Thankfully, there were still several species of fish available that could fill the requirements including ladyfish, sheepshead, spotted seatrout, and southern flounder.

We were fishing with Dolphin Dock's charter in Port Aransas, Texas. A boat captain indicated they were catching gafftopsail catfish. This was another fish species that would complete Karen's elite angler qualification. To qualify for the big fish award, she needed the fish to be at least 20 inches in length. We were hopeful for positive results since we had fished with the Dolphin Docks crew many times before and had achieved both state and waterbody records.

Throughout the day, we each caught several hardhead catfish, sand seatrout, and small gafftopsail catfish, but the big fish still eluded Karen. Several anglers on the boat started landing big gafftopsail catfish, and Karen's frustration level increased as my 21.5-inch gafftopsail catfish cleared the gunnel. You could see her intensity building as she landed another hardhead catfish. She quickly rebaited her hook with a piece of cut bait topped with a shrimp and dropped her line over the side. It was only a few moments later when her rod bent over hard. This was not a hardhead catfish.

Captain Tim watched intently as she fought the fish. He knew Karen was after a record fish and he worked hard to put her in a position to get one. Karen moved past me to the back of the boat and landed a 22-inch gafftopsail catfish completing her saltwater elite angler award qualification. After returning to the dock, we weighed the fish. Along with her elite angler award qualification, the 3.56-pound fish set the waterbody record for the bay. We were grateful for another notable, enjoyable trip.

Several anglers have informed me the reason they do not record records is that they do not know where to find an approved scale. States vary on the type of scale and weighing method required to approve a record. Many states provide a list of locations that maintain a scale that can be used for weighing potential record fish. Marinas often have scales that are accepted by the state fish and wildlife department. Local feed stores and butcher shops may also have scales that can be used to weigh record catches.

DOCUMENTATION | 27

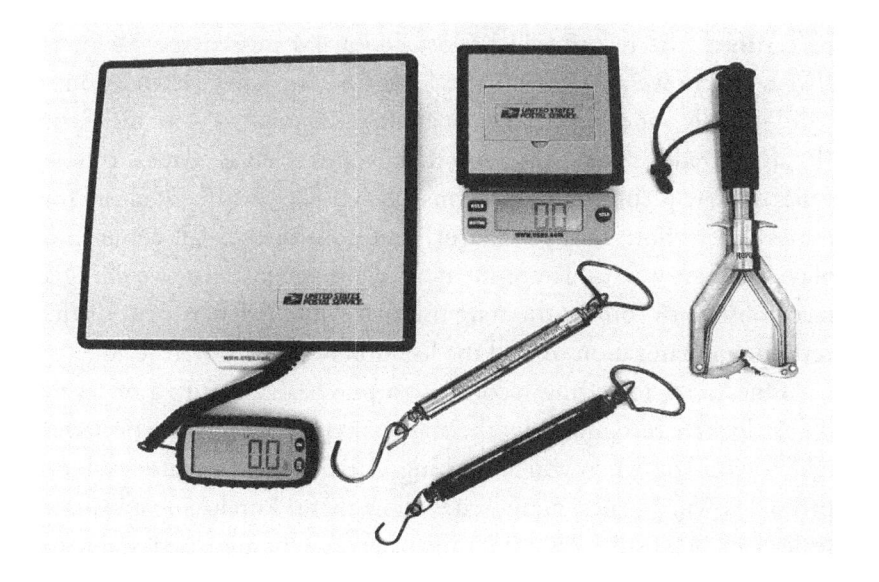

Potentially certifiable scales come in several types including hanging and floor models like this 300-pound digital scale, 10-pound digital scale, Rapala Lock'n Weigh device, and 12-pound and 25-pound Chatillon hanging scales.

The date a scale is certified is often mandatory on the record application form. Therefore, make sure you obtain this information when you weigh your fish. Several states require scales to be certified every year or two. The IGFA mandates that a scale is certified every 12 months. If a fish is weighed on a scale that has not been certified, some organizations may allow the scale to be certified after a fish is caught and weighed. However, if this scale is submitted and cannot be certified, the record will be lost. To avoid missed records, it is always best to weigh a fish on a scale that has an active certification.

Typically, adequate scales are either defined as "certified" or "legal-for-trade" scales. The terminology and science related to how scales operate is complicated. Terms like sensitivity drift, IP rating for ingress protection, hysteresis error, and non-linearity all come into play. The best way to determine if a scale is adequate for weighing a record fish is to contact the state fish and wildlife department or the certifying organization to find the location of an approved scale.

One secret to setting records is to purchase a certified or legal-for-trade scale recognized by the state or certifying organization and take it with you when you are fishing. Although some states exclude privately owned scales, many states allow them. Purchasing adequate scales can be costly. Pay attention when purchasing used scales to ensure the scale's certification has not expired since certification can cost as much as a used scale. For members, the IGFA will certify scales up to 100 pounds for a fee. An IGFA certification is accepted by many states and record keeping organizations.

There are several sizes and types of scales available and selecting the best scale depends on the type of fish being weighed. A ten-pound scale is adequate for many fish species. For larger fish, I own a certified scale that can weigh up to 300 pounds in tenth-pound increments. Several brands of scales are battery operated so you can carry them while fishing. Spring driven handheld scales are the most common scales utilized by anglers however digital scales may produce more accurate results. Conduct thorough research to choose the proper scale to meet your needs. The IGFA publishes the top ten scales used to record world records in their annual record publication.

Always zero a scale when a holding device is used to document weight. A plastic sheet was placed on the scale, and the scale was "zeroed." This unrestricted category Texas state record blue tilapia was added to obtain a weight of 4 pounds 8.8 ounces or 4.55 pounds.

My wife and I normally carry two scales in a padded, water resistant laptop computer bag when fishing. One scale weighs up to ten pounds, and the other weighs up to 300 pounds. Although a ten-pound scale may be all that is needed on a fishing excursion, carrying this small scale into the backcountry can still be awkward. Normally you will not catch a fish exceeding 300-pounds. If you do, you will usually be saltwater fishing and can locate a marina that has a certified scale. If you are freshwater fishing and catch a fish over 300 pounds, you will receive attention and assistance to locate a certified scale.

The best part about taking an approved certified scale with you is you can keep a fish alive and still obtain the required information for a record. When you weigh a fish, documentation should include multiple photographs of the fish on a scale with the weight display clearly visible. On digital scales, reflections can make it impossible to see the weight display in a picture so be careful to avoid this situation.

For floor scales, a bucket or board can be used to hold a fish during weighing. Be sure to "zero" a scale first with a holding device placed on the scale. A picture should be taken to indicate the holding device is not included with the weight of the fish. By taking time to include key information, like a picture of a zero on the scale with the holding device in place, a certifying agency will be more willing to approve a record without requiring additional information.

Be cognizant of weight increments and measurement types a scale utilizes. Many scales measure in pounds with decimal pounds, but scales can also measure in pounds and ounces. Others weigh in kilograms. Make sure the weight on a scale matches or is converted to the weight type on a record submittal form. Conversion programs are available online. The IGFA requires weight to be reported in the increments shown on the scale during weighing, so do not convert the data for IGFA world records.

Be aware of a scale's accuracy and if possible use a scale that has a measuring range close to the size of the fish you are weighing. If you are weighing a one pound fish, you will receive a more accurate weight if you weigh the fish on a ten-pound scale that weighs in 0.1 ounce increments compared to a 500 pound scale that weighs in 0.2

pound (3.2 ounce) increments. A couple of ounces can make a big difference if you are trying to replace an existing record, especially for small fish species. On one occasion, I was able to use my certified ten-pound scale to allow an angler to replace an existing state vermilion snapper record by just 0.1 ounces. He had originally weighed the fish on a larger scale that indicated the fish was short of the record by approximately one ounce. He had been trying to achieve this record for years and was excited to obtain recognition for his catch.

Remember that some states only allow fish to be weighed at a specific location. Other states and the FFHF require two witnesses to observe a weighing. Some states require that a state fish and wildlife department employee be present during weighing. Most record-keeping organizations require an angler to provide the name, address, and phone number of a person weighing the fish. Other standards may apply so check all requirements carefully. In general, a record fish that is weighed and harvested should be frozen and kept until the record is approved. Although a fish will lose weight in a freezer, it is better to have the fish available in case further confirmation is needed.

The IGFA requires fish to be weighed on land. This protocol ensures weight accuracy. Weights taken at sea or on any body of water will not be accepted. Many world records have been lost from anglers weighing a fish in a floating boat, on a boat tied to a dock, or by weighing a fish on a floating marina. The IGFA also requires the person weighing the fish to see the rod and reel used to make the catch. Always be aware of the rules, take pictures, and capture witnesses who are present during the weighing process.

- MEASUREMENTS -

Our family was anchored near a channel in the Florida Keys enjoying a day of fishing. We had already created many wonderful memories on this fishing trip by catching dolphin, blackfin tuna, gray snapper, mutton snapper, great barracuda, and red grouper with several other species landed throughout the week. We decided to stop fishing offshore and headed inshore with hopes of catching a tarpon.

My daughter Cindy and her husband Rudy were visiting when the back rod on our boat bent parallel to the water, and the Penn International 12 reel started screaming as line flew off it. It was Rudy's turn on the rod. After the initial fish's run, the line was coming off the reel steadily. A few minutes went by and based on the way the fish was fighting it was not acting like a tarpon. The fight was long and hard as Rudy cranked the handle on the reel in a back and forth battle. The fish was staying in the general area, but it did not give up much ground. Finally, the fish started tiring, and Rudy was happy to retrieve some line. The fish swam behind the stern of the boat, and the line slowly began rising. Rolling near the surface, the fish came into clear view. It was an enormous nurse shark! Strategically, Rudy brought the monster nurse shark along the side of the boat. The fish easily dwarfed my 48-inch measuring board. Fortunately, the nurse shark was exhausted allowing us to take an accurate measurement while leaving the fish in the water beside the boat. A construction retractable steel tape confirmed the measurement at nine feet eight inches. Although the shark was not harvested to determine if it was a record, it was an amazing fish. We all reveled in the catch as we revived the fish, released it, and watched it swim away.

Measuring device requirements used to document record fish vary greatly between states and organizations. Several states require a solid or metal ruler. Measurements with cloth or plastic tapes are often not accepted. You should have a quick estimating device and an accurate measuring device for measuring potential record fish. A quick measurement device can be as simple as using a plastic sewing tape. This is an inexpensive option and can be found at most stores. Even if you are not able to use this type of tape as an approved measuring device, it will provide a rapid measurement to determine if you need to get an official measuring board, saving you fishing time.

Another useful method is to place measuring tape on your fishing rod. Commercial measuring stickers for fishing rods are available from several stores that carry fishing tackle. There are even measuring stickers you can place on the outside of your boat. These stickers are great for acquiring quick measurements and in some circumstances

Big fish require a retractable construction tape measuring device to obtain an accurate measurement. Rudy Garza landed this giant nurse shark measuring nine feet eight inches, much longer than most measuring boards.

can be used for an accurate measurement of a large fish allowing you to keep the fish in the water. The difficult part is getting a good picture of the fish's length or a picture of an angler with the fish.

A 48-inch measuring board is an excellent tool for measuring fish. Mine is made of wood and has an aluminum measuring stick inlaid into the board. The board has a perpendicular extension at one end allowing the fish's nose to be placed against the extension for an accurate measurement. A 48-inch measuring board is appropriate for 90 percent of fish commonly caught. A metric version of this type of board is utilized by biologists for recording fish lengths. Small boards of similar design can be purchased at tackle stores. My 48-inch board is large and awkward to carry, but it provides an accurate measurement and does a great job of holding small fish for pictures. If you make a board, it needs to be waterproof and easy to clean.

Carrying a 12-foot retractable construction tape measuring device is valuable in case you catch a really big fish. Fortunately, there have been several occasions when my 48-inch measuring board was not long enough to measure my catch. If you use a retractable tape be precise and take accurate measurements since the tape does not have a stop for the nose of the fish. Pushing the tape against a wall or the side of the boat can accomplish the same purpose. Take a picture when you measure a fish and make sure you can see the entire length of the fish on the measuring device. At least one picture should show the head of the fish with the mouth closed touching the perpendicular stop. Also, zoom in on the measuring device, so the fish measurement number is clearly visible and can be easily read.

Fish are measured in several ways. The two most popular methods are total length and fork length. Total length is usually calculated by placing a fish on a flat surface with the jaw closed and measuring the fish's length while manipulating the tail fin to achieve the maximum length possible. Fork length is determined by placing a fish on a flat surface with the jaw closed and measuring to the fork of the tail. Fork length can be considerably shorter than total length. Most states require measurements using total length. Fork length is often used in federal offshore waters for species such as billfish. For world records

DOCUMENTATION | 35

Measuring boards provide an accurate way to determine the length of fish. This 19-inch sheepshead is a waterbody record.

the IGFA uses fork length measurements while the FFHF requires total length measurements. Verify the correct method required by the certifying organization before submitting your record. Be sure to utilize the most recent regulations from the organization, and stay abreast of changes to help you avoid a lost record.

The IGFA mandates that potential world record catch and release fish be measured on an official IGFA length measuring device. Other devices are not accepted for measuring the length of record fish for world records certified by the IGFA. An IGFA measuring device can be acquired online at igfa.org and measures fish using the metric system. Since many anglers do not own this device, purchasing one provides an angler with an advantage to set length world records.

While it is often not required to obtain a record many state fish and wildlife departments, as well as the IGFA and FFHF, request the girth of a fish to be documented in their record applications. The girth of a fish is the largest measurement around the fish's body at the biggest point. Depending on the fish species this measurement can be taken in the middle of the body or closer to the head. Fish girth provides valuable data concerning a fish's condition and weight. Sewing tape, fishing line, or string are all adequate tools to measure girth. To obtain a girth measurement, wrap a piece of fishing line around a fish, mark it, and lay it on a measuring board. Do not pull the line too tight to ensure an accurate measurement.

The most frequent mistake when measuring a fish is to measure the fish along the contour of the fish's body. This form of measurement is called curve length. Although this may provide a much longer fish length than a total length measurement, it is often not the correct method for measuring fish, and it can disqualify a record.

Record certifying organizations usually mandate that fish are measured while lying on a flat surface. If there is not a measuring board available, then place a fish on the ground or on the bottom of a boat while taking measurements. Measuring a fish along the contour of the fish's body can result in a violation of existing regulations. Therefore, make sure you understand the regulatory agency's rules before measuring your fish.

DOCUMENTATION | 37

An official IGFA measuring device must be purchased and utilized to document an IGFA all-tackle length world record. Although this largemouth bass was not a world record, it was a waterbody catch and release record.

Another common mistake is leaving a fish's mouth open when measurements are taken. A gaping mouth on a big fish may add several inches to the measurement and is not acceptable. This type of measurement can result in a violation of state regulations since a fish may not meet mandated length restrictions. For world record length measurements, the IGFA requires a picture that clearly shows a fish's mouth closed and pressed against the perpendicular end of an IGFA official measuring device.

One secret to acquiring records is to take accurate measurements. Do not round down unless you are required to do so. If the fish you catch is five feet, one and one-half inches (61.5 inches) in length do not report the fish as five feet (60 inches) or even as five feet one inch (61 inches). A half inch can make a major difference in maintaining your record if another angler attempts to replace it. Accurate measurements are especially important for small fish species such as bluegill. Conversely, do not round measurements up to the next big break such as reporting a fish that is 59 inches in length as a five foot fish (60 inches). A legitimate record of another angler should not be lost due to improper reporting and rounding.

- PHOTOGRAPHS -

The aqua blue water turned to a royal blue as we trolled off the reef into 100 feet of water. My wife Karen, daughter Cindy, and I rented a 23-foot boat to fish in the Florida Keys. The seas were around two feet, and the jet-head lures were running perfectly behind our boat. We were trolling for about 30 minutes when my daughter yelled "Sailfish!" A beautiful sailfish was repeatedly busting out of the water, and it was my turn on the rod. The boat dropped off plane as the throttle was placed in neutral. The sailfish flew wildly into the air trying to dislodge the lure as I took the rod from the holder.

Cindy decided to take a video on our digital camera as the sailfish continued jumping. The fish dove deep momentarily before bursting through the surface several more times. The fish was an amazing jumper and quickly wore itself out with all the acrobatics. As I pulled the sailfish alongside the boat, Cindy switched the camera from video to picture mode to acquire some still shots. She took some stunning pictures including me with the sailfish.

We were all excited to see the video of the fish. That night we hooked up the camera and saw 30 seconds of the fight, then darkness. Cindy did not know that my camera was an older model that only recorded 30 seconds of video at a time. Fortunately, although we lost the video, we still had several striking pictures of the fish.

Photographic errors are one of the most common ways to lose a record. Almost every state requires photographic evidence of a potential record fish. Pictures serve to verify your catch and obtain proper identification of the fish species. As a general rule, take lots of pictures and use more than one camera as a safety measure.

Several types of cameras and video equipment have been part of my gear over the years and have provided adequate pictures to document my fishing experiences. A small Kodak digital twelve-megapixel camera has served me well, when fishing in both freshwater and saltwater, to document my record catches. Originally an old six-megapixel camera was used, but it produced grainy pictures. If you want to enlarge your photographs, you may need a higher resolution camera. Camera quality is continually improving, and poor resolution is becoming less of an issue for record documentation.

Many phones are equipped with high-resolution cameras to record a record catch. When internet service is available, utilizing a phone to take pictures can provide the advantage of being able to immediately email a picture to a safe location. Fishing sites are often located in harsh environments, and an angler must decide if exposing a phone to the elements is worth the potential damage.

No matter what type of camera you use, it is important to keep the camera lens clean. Water, blood, or gunk splashed on the lens can result in pictures that are unusable in verifying a record catch. While taking a picture of a large common carp, Karen's last fish for her freshwater elite angler award, we did not realize there was a smudge on the camera lens. Landing the fish resulted in Karen being the first woman in Texas to achieve both the Texas Parks and Wildlife Department

Freshwater and Saltwater Elite Angler Awards, so it was an important fish. Although the pictures were acceptable for verification, the quality was not acceptable to allow Karen's fish to be posted as the fish of the month on the state's website. Using two cameras would have solved this issue. Since this mishap I learned my lesson, and using two cameras has saved a record on multiple occasions.

Utilize the video camera mode to record your fishing adventures. A video not only provides great memories but can also be used to further document your catch, especially if you are using a method of fishing other than a traditional rod and reel. High definition quality video cameras are becoming more popular, and many are now waterproof providing excellent video quality and additional safety measures against the elements. Remember that some states will not accept video as the only documentation of your record, so be sure to take still pictures as well. Check the camera mode when you start taking pictures of your catch and determine the desired mode for the situation. If your camera is in the wrong mode, your picture may be blurry or display the wrong color tone.

You should always take standard pictures of your catch including a picture of you with your fish, a picture of your fish on a measuring device, and a picture of your fish on a scale with the weight visible. When photographing your fish length and weight take a picture that shows the entire fish in the photograph. Be sure to take a close-up picture of your fish on a scale and measuring device to document the values for the length and weight. It is a good idea to take pictures of spectators and witnesses to support verification of the catch.

Take at least one great close up picture of you and your fish for enjoyment value as well as documentation. If this picture is of suitable quality, it could be used in publications giving you additional recognition. When you take a picture, a fish should be held far enough away from your body to show its proper size. Do not hold the fish too far away from your body because this will make your picture look out of proportion to the fish's actual size. If the fish looks much larger than it really is, this will diminish picture quality, and it will appear as if you are trying to exaggerate the size of the fish.

For most fish species a picture showing the side of a fish is all that is necessary for identification. For other species of fish, pictures showing further detail may be required. For example, one difference between a common carp and a smallmouth buffalo is the presence of barbels on the common carp. The barbels are the small projections that come off the side of a carp's mouth, so make sure to take a picture of a carp's head for identification purposes.

One difference between black crappie and white crappie is the number of dorsal spines on the top fin of the fish. Therefore include a picture of a crappie's dorsal fin fully extended, so the number of dorsal spines is visible. For freshwater catfish, a picture of the rays of the anal fin can be used to separate blue catfish from channel catfish. Take a picture of the anal fin when documenting a record freshwater catfish. For unusual saltwater species or for species difficult to identify, take several pictures.

For sharks and other hard to identify species pictures should be taken of the head, tail, belly, dorsal fin, mouth, teeth, and anal fin. Pictures of a shark's teeth are particularly important because, in some cases, a shark can be identified using only pictures of its teeth. Even though several pictures are taken only one or two may end up being utilized in identifying a fish species.

Ample photographic evidence is required to readily identify your fish and separate it from other closely related species. If you harvest a fish and retain it, photographic evidence is not as critical but for catch and release records your initial pictures may be the only evidence available to document your record.

If you do harvest a fish, keep it frozen until you receive notification of your record. If you destroy your fish and an issue develops you may lose your record. Most states indicate that if a fish cannot be positively identified, then the record will be lost.

Always check your camera and be aware of objects affecting the picture. My camera is usually carried in a zip-lock bag for protection from water damage while fishing. During a fishing trip, a whale shark swam up to the boat just a few feet below the surface. Several pictures of the fish were taken before the whale shark swam away.

Unfortunately, when the camera was removed from the zip-lock bag, I held it between my fingers to get it out of the way. Unbeknownst to me, part of the bag was covering my camera lens. Therefore my treasured rare pictures of a whale shark in the Gulf of Mexico will forever have a blurred plastic bag in the foreground.

The lens cover, fingers, clothes, background objects, and sun direction can all destroy a picture and cause the loss of a record. On a sunny day, always try to take pictures with the sun behind you and on your subject. Be aware of shadows on your subject when taking a photograph. Hold your camera still and make sure your subject is in focus. Many cameras have a focus indicator, but a sudden movement when taking your picture can still cause blurring to occur. During the excitement after you catch a record fish, it is easy to forget the photographic basics, so pay attention beforehand to get a great picture.

When taking a picture of an angler with a fish, the fish's orientation is very important for aesthetics and documenting your record. If a fish is flopping or jumping, you may end up with a picture of a blurred fish. For record documentation purposes an angler should hold a fish so that the entire side of the fish is visible.

Do not take a picture looking straight at a fish's belly since this may result in the fish appearing to be a large white blob. Usually, a fish picture will look better if the fish is held parallel to the ground. Having two people hold a large fish provides perspective and shows off the size of the fish. If you place a fish on the ground or on the deck of a boat make sure to place a familiar object next to the fish to give the viewer context to determine its actual size. Without an object next to the fish, it may appear to be very small.

Forgetting a camera or having dead batteries can result in a catastrophic trip from a record standpoint. Carry extra batteries and make a list of the proper camera equipment needed for your trip. If your camera is rechargeable make sure it is fully charged before every outing. It is also a great idea to take a phone charger so you can use your phone as a backup device when taking pictures. If you lose your camera or the removable data card, your pictures may be lost along with your record catch. Download your pictures on a computer as soon as possible to back them up in more than one location. You should also have an extra camera stored on the boat or in the car for impromptu fishing trips. I cannot overstress how many records have been lost due to the lack of proper photographic documentation.

- SMARTPHONES -

The mosaic of turquoise water and dark patches indicated we were trolling over areas of coral reef scattered across a sandy bottom, a perfect location to catch great barracuda. We were fishing in Islamorada, Florida, and my wife Karen landed a nice Spanish mackerel. My daughter, Laura, and her husband, Doug, were putting out trolling lines alternating between a blue and white jet-head, a six-inch purple Yo-Zuri bonito lure, a dolphin colored cedar plug, and a small pink squid lure. Doug was next on the rod.

On this trolling pass, the pink squid lure was the winner. The rod suddenly bent over hard, and the screaming reel was answered with the call, "Fish on!" from all quarters. Doug picked up the rod and disengaged the clicker. He is an experienced angler and began skillfully working the fish towards the boat. The great barracuda was large, feisty, and had an attitude.

Doug was relentless, and after a good fight, he brought the fish to the gaff. It was a large great barracuda estimated to weigh over 40 pounds. Doug held up the fish for a picture. There were several people on the boat, and when I turned around, it looked like paparazzi finding a celebrity. Flashes rapidly went off, and everyone was positioning for the best photo opportunity. Losing this memory was not going to occur on this occasion.

Smartphones are readily accessible and make it easier to capture quality pictures in any scenario. Not only can you obtain an excellent photograph, if service is available you can save an image to more than one location. Although pictures taken with a smartphone may not produce the same high-quality images as those taken with a single purpose camera, they are usually suitable for documenting a record. Technological advances are furthering smartphone capabilities.

44 | THE ART OF FISHING FOR RECORDS

Make sure the lens on your camera is clean and not obstructed when you snap a picture. You do not want to lose a potential record for a fish like Doug Mosley's massive great barracuda.

Smartphones are terrific for checking records since anglers can search the internet to identify unknown species, review data forms, and brag about a catch. On more than one occasion my smartphone was used to take a picture of a record fish when my digital camera did not function properly.

There are a variety of applications (apps) and programs that have been developed to assist in fishing and collecting data during fishing excursions. Apps provide information on weather conditions, navigation, fishing structure, bait selection, and the best time of year to fish. Apps are available for estimating fish weight and length. Apps can give specific information on fishing locations such as water release data, the locations where fish are currently being caught, and what type of insect hatch is occurring. There are even apps to connect a smartphone to an alarm on your rod that will alert you when you get a bite. The IGFA has an app available to check fishing records in real time. This app is a wonderful tool for anglers as it provides a variety of information including world record information, weight station locations, quest lists, rules, contact information, and species identification. Several fish and wildlife departments have their own apps.

Guides use smartphones to increase catch rates especially in freshwater where cellular service is readily available. Guides often talk to each other about where fish are biting, what they are biting, and how deep the water is where fish are being caught. There are pros and cons to this activity. During several guided trips, my guide spent a great deal of time on his phone gathering information. Although utilizing a phone may assist in catching fish, it can distract from your fishing experience if a guide, or someone else, uses a phone excessively.

Although technology has increased our knowledge and understanding of fishing, do not let technology distract from your fishing experiences. Fishing can provide quality time and personal interaction with other anglers and family members leading to lifelong memories. Do not waste opportunities to build relationships by staying addicted to your electronic devices. Spending the day fishing with someone who is obsessed with social media and technology takes away from the fishing experience. If you are fishing on my boat and you are constantly tweeting, blogging, texting, etc., your phone may be confiscated. The phone light app will be turned on (in the green color mode if you have it) and I will tie your phone to my line as a fish attractor…but then I am old school.

- WITNESSES -

The sunshine felt warm against my skin on the cool December morning. Common carp were rolling on the surface of the lake slowly feeding around floating logs and debris. Most of the carp were around 20 inches in length, but a large swirl made me believe there was a trophy fish mixed within the group. With one of my favorite Browning fly rods in hand, the elk hair fly tied on a number two hook was ready to be thrown in any direction if a big common carp was spotted. A large shape moved below the water's surface, and my cast placed the fly a few inches directly in front of the fish. The fish did not have to change its speed as it slowly rose toward the fly. Anticipating the fish eating the fly, my fly rod was already moving backward in the process of setting the hook as the fish engulfed it. The rod stopped when the fish was hooked. The fly reel immediately gave up the fly line and most of the backing.

Several people from the lake marina formed a crowd and cheered me on as I continued to reel in the fish. The fish was strong for a common carp, and it took several minutes before the fish swam into the net. Immediately a person exclaimed, "Oh it's just a trash carp." It was a common carp, but it was a large one at 30 inches in length and a lake waterbody record on a fly rod.

Even though people are often near the area where I am fishing, fishing alone is a common occurrence for me, and the lack of a witness can be an issue when catching record fish. Regulations concerning witnesses vary greatly between organizations. Read the regulations concerning witnesses carefully. My wife Karen enjoys fishing with me and has been a witness on several occasions since some states allow a relative to be a witness. Others states and organizations do not allow a relative to be a witness for documentation purposes. Many states

DOCUMENTATION | 47

Locating adequate witnesses can result in acquiring various types of records including world, state, and multi-species records.

require at least two witnesses to sign a fish record submittal form. State agencies may also mandate that a witness be present when a fish is weighed and measured.

For freshwater world records the FFHF requests two disinterested witnesses to observe a fish being weighed. An applicant is not allowed to be one of those witnesses. The IGFA requests two witnesses to observe a catch other than an angler or a captain, and one witness other than an angler, a captain, or a weighmaster to observe the weighing process.

Finding a witness can be a challenge when catching a record. In today's world, most people will not provide private information such as their address or phone number on a form given to them by a stranger. If you find bystanders willing to be witnesses ensure they agree with the information submitted on the form from the approving agency concerning the record catch. Carry additional submittal forms and provide your witnesses with a draft copy. This copy can be used as a reference if witnesses are contacted by a certifying agency. For anglers who are serious about setting records, it is best to fish with someone who can serve as a witness.

In some cases, a video can be used to document your catch. However, certain organizations will not accept a video as the only documentation of a record. If witnesses are not available, and if allowed, you can film yourself fighting a fish as documentation. Fighting a fish at the same time you are trying to video a catch can be a risky endeavor, but it is possible. You must weigh the risk of losing your fish against the benefits of properly documenting a catch. Some video cameras allow for hands-free operation making filming easier.

Although a certifying agency may not accept a video as the sole source for a record, a video will definitely help in determining if a record can be certified. Depending on the fish and wildlife department, a video may replace a witness if one is not available. Provide your video to the state fish and wildlife department along with your other submittal information and ask for a ruling. If possible, video yourself with a fish on the line including the fishing equipment you are using. If you apply this technique, make sure to turn the video

DOCUMENTATION | 49

Obtaining witnesses can be difficult when documenting a record. Captain Clay Yadon, Reel Deal Lake Whitney Striper Guide, was helpful when witnessing the weighing of Barry Osborn's unrestricted Texas state record and FFHF world record 10.75-pound striper acquired using the Plnor fishing method.

camera toward yourself to show you are the angler catching the fish. The IGFA record submittal form has a space to indicate whether or not a video of a catch was created.

When you fill out a submittal form for your record, be sure to indicate in the witness section that the enclosed video constitutes your witness information. It will be a waiting game to see what response you will receive from the fish and wildlife department. In general, people from state departments make proper decisions when given a chance. However, if the rules specifically indicate that a witness must be present during the catch, you may lose your record. Many states regulate their award programs through a committee to review record disputes. Their decision is usually final. The IGFA and FFHF provide dispute resolution information on their websites.

When striving for a record, there are details and rules to remember, but the process gets easier the more records you achieve. Learning the art of fishing for records requires effort, but you will be glad you invested time once you see your name in record archives. It is fun to look back at your records and remember the experiences years later.

3

RECORDS AND RECOGNITION

- WORLD RECORDS -

The large dark tail of a feeding fish could be distinguished in the muddy brown water. A year had passed since a similar situation had occurred and this time I was ready for the event. I ran to the van to retrieve my fly rod rigged with IGFA rated fly line. The elk hair sinking fly on a number two Mustad hook was tied to a 20-pound tippet. The fly rod and reel were in compliance with IGFA world record regulations. When I reached the shore, the situation was unchanged, and the fly sank in the water just to the side of the fish's tail. Only seconds passed before the line tightened. The hook set was strong as the fish headed for deep water. My heart sank when I felt the drag on the line as the fish swam over a rock. The fight wore on, and somehow the frayed line never broke. Finally, the fish came free from the rock and moved toward the shore. The net slid under the fish, and the large smallmouth buffalo was lifted from the water. It was several months before the IGFA approved the 13 pound 7-ounce fish as the new 20-pound tippet class world record. My preparation paid off.

The smallmouth buffalo catch was almost exactly like a catch from the year before. Water clarity, location, and the species of fish were all the same. The difference in achieving this world record was in understanding the rules and equipment needed. The pending IGFA record was checked. The line was tested for the correct breaking strength, and the fly rod and fly both met the required specifications. Because of my preparation, the fishing event ended as anticipated and resulted in a world record catch.

Although several organizations maintain world records, the IGFA is recognized as the leading authority for documenting freshwater and saltwater world records. The IGFA was founded in 1939 and has representatives in 88 countries and territories. This organization has spent years developing a fair set of worldwide angling rules. Because of this effort, there are very specific rules that apply to IGFA world record catches. Tournament organizations often utilize the IGFA's rules and millions of dollars in tournament prize money have been lost by anglers that did not follow the rules.

The IGFA only maintains rod and reel records, including fly fishing records. Fish must weigh a minimum of one pound to qualify. The IGFA added a catch and release program in 2011 for all-tackle length records for specific fish species. The rod, reel, and line all have rules governing what qualifies as a legal fishing method. For certain species of fish, records are broken into line class and tippet class categories for fly fishing. There are restrictions regarding line types, leaders, hooks, lures, and the methods applied when fighting a fish. There are also restrictions concerning fighting chairs, gimbals, gaffs, nets, and other equipment. An angler must adhere to IGFA rules during the hook-up, the fight, and the landing of a fish. Otherwise, an angler's catch will be disqualified. Because many of the techniques described in this book do not use a rod and reel, these methods will eliminate your chances of catching an IGFA world record.

In addition to fishing records, the IGFA maintains a fishing hall of fame and museum. This allows the organization to implement part of their mission to provide outstanding recognition and accomplishments in the field of angling. Induction into the IGFA hall of fame is a major form of recognition resulting in a chance to be honored and respected as a participant in angling history on a worldwide level.

Freshwater world records are also documented by the Fresh Water Fishing Hall of Fame (FFHF) and Museum in Hayward, Wisconsin. The original idea for the FFHF started in 1960 and expanded in 1969,

RECORDS AND RECOGNITION | 53

If you take the time to understand the rules, achieving a world record is easier than you might think. This average sized 10.0-pound common carp caught by Karen Osborn is the 30-pound line class IGFA world record.

1972, and 1976 with the opening of a museum facility. A catch and release program was added in 1993. In addition to recording records, the FFHF maintains an enshrinement program providing recognition in several categories. Noteworthy information can be obtained at freshwater-fishing.org. Induction into the Fresh Water Fishing Hall of Fame and Museum results in worldwide recognition and the chance to be enshrined in freshwater fishing history for endeavors that have a national or worldwide impact to the sport of fishing.

While both the FFHF and the IGFA maintain rod and reel world records for freshwater fish, the FFHF expands freshwater world record opportunities by maintaining records for categories other than rod and reel. Besides all-tackle freshwater world records, the FFHF documents world records in four divisions including rod and reel, pole and line no reel, fly fishing, and ice fishing.

FFHF world records are separated into North American world records and foreign world records. In addition to all-tackle records for freshwater fish, the FFHF maintains records for line class and tippet class categories greatly expanding an angler's chances to receive a freshwater world record. Unlike the IGFA where the largest line class allowed is 130 pounds and the largest tippet class is 20 pounds, the FFHF has an unlimited line and tippet category allowing for records on any size line or tippet.

Preparation is important in catching a record fish. Although many state records do not require much preparation from an equipment standpoint, equipment is extremely important when trying to set an IGFA or FFHF world record. A fish caught on a 12-pound tippet may qualify as a tippet class world record, but the same fish may not qualify as a world record if caught using an 8-pound tippet. In many cases, heavier or longer fish records exist for fish caught using a smaller tippet or line class.

Reviewing record categories and existing records can help you select the best equipment to set a world record. There are separate IGFA categories for men and women anglers, so review existing IGFA world records carefully to identify the right equipment to increase your chances for a record for a specific fish species.

World records and especially all-tackle world records are often considered the highest level of angling record achievement. Because the rules continually change, specific IGFA and FFHF rules will not be discussed in this book. If you are interested in catching an IGFA world record review the rules on the IGFA website at igfa.org. To evaluate freshwater world records, the FFHF rules can be obtained at freshwater-fishing.org. There are fees associated with gaining membership and applying for world records with both the IGFA and the FFHF. This money is used to enhance the sport of fishing. Take the time to visit a hall of fame and museum to see the history of the sport and to envision your place in fishing history and lore. Remember every time you cast a hook you could catch a new world record fish.

- STATE RECORDS -

The birds were scattered and feeding heavily on bait balls located a few miles in front of the jetty. Most of the fish were average to small size Spanish mackerel. I was fishing with my wife Karen and our friends Ken and Kim. We landed several Spanish mackerel, and we were enjoying a fun-filled morning. Ken was still giggling as usual when he threw another Spanish mackerel into the boat. Ken is a big kid at heart, and he loves catching Spanish mackerel.

We were floating toward a bait ball. Casting my rod, the gold spoon lure glimmered as it sailed over the blue water. The heavy handmade spoon went past the bait ball splashing as it broke the surface. The retrieve was sporadic. A small fish hit the lure but released itself with a quick head shake. Because the fishless lure was past the bait ball, I reeled it quickly. The lure never made it back to the boat. A fish hit hard and headed for the front of the boat. The fish was smoking line off the reel. Moving past the other anglers my goal was to make my way to the bow. The fish was fighting like a big king mackerel. The fish slowed down, and the light drag on the reel kept the hook from pulling from its soft mouth. Only a small amount of line remained on the Garcia Ambassador 6500 reel but the fish eventually stopped, and the line retrieval commenced. Finally, the fish was coaxed to the boat, and to my surprise, it turned out to be a huge Spanish mackerel instead of a king mackerel. Karen realized it might be a record and grabbed the camera. The fish was lifted into the boat and held against the measuring board. Karen took several quick pictures of the fish on the board and a few of me holding it. The fish was then quickly dropped over the side, and we watched it swim away. The 28.25-inch Spanish mackerel was later certified as the Texas catch and release state record. The record remained the state record for five years until it was replaced by a longer Spanish mackerel.

Most states post fishing records on their websites based on weight. Many anglers never search beyond the weight record category to determine if other categories are available. States may recognize a variety of record categories including catch and release, bowfishing, fly fishing, and other unconventional methods. Catch and release records are usually based on length instead of weight.

Some states allow records to be recorded for any fish species while other states restrict fish records to a specific list of fish. Anglers often become aware of fishing record programs by catching a large fish and researching the rules to document the record. Once an angler realizes that it is not difficult to catch and record a record fish, they will often work to achieve more than one record catch. Therefore, several states have anglers with multiple records documented including several different species. It is interesting to look at a state's fishing record history to identify when an angler became interested in recording records. An angler may document records for a few years before losing interest, moving from the state where records were achieved, or deciding to discontinue submitting records. Other anglers begin recording records as junior anglers and document records for many years.

Since fishing records have been maintained by most states for decades, an angler might conclude that it is impossible to achieve a new state record. However, this is not the case. New state fishing records are achieved every year in several categories for a variety of fish species. Due to the rising interest in fishing, and the desire of anglers to earn fishing records, many states are expanding their record programs. Enthusiastic anglers are joining the sport everyday.

Data analysis is not the goal of this book. However, Table 1 shows 51 of my active state records posted on August 2, 2018, from the Texas Parks and Wildlife Department website at tpwd.texas.gov. These 51 state records were obtained between October 15, 2010, and July 1, 2018. Texas has a robust fishing record program, and Table 1 is an example of the vast number of species available. Since there are a greater amount of fish species in saltwater, saltwater fishing can increase the chances of setting a record. Table 1 demonstrates this fact since thirty-two fish (63%) are saltwater records.

Table 1 also shows that other methods of fishing besides using a rod and reel can enhance the possibility of setting a record. Twenty-seven (53%) of the fish records are other methods category pole and line no reel (Plnor) or handline records. Nine of the records (18%) are catch and release records. Excluding the three fish taken with a bow and arrow, twenty-two of the fish records (46%) are records obtained using artificial lures, including fourteen records (29%) on a fly. Three (6%) of the records are bow and arrow category records. Most anglers concentrate on fishing for a few fish species, but as Table 1 indicates there are a vast number and variety of state records an angler can procure from a state with a robust record program in just seven years.

Based on this data, there are multiple points to consider. Some of the records shown are for short and light fish that can easily be replaced. Other fish like the cobia, little tunny, and remora received two state records in different categories. Some species such as the stingrays and sharks were difficult to identify and needed multiple pictures to be verified by an ichthyologist. Ensure adequate information is collected for identification purposes.

When trying to achieve records, anglers have a tendency to concentrate on big species of fish such as billfish, sharks, and tuna. However, by taking this stance, anglers will miss out on extensive record opportunities available in both freshwater and saltwater categories. Although there is a vast difference between fighting a 1,200-pound tiger shark in comparison to fighting a 0.5-pound sand perch, the state records will be listed the same way. Both anglers will be able to proudly proclaim they caught a state record fish.

- TABLE 1 -

Fifty-one state fish records achieved by Barry Osborn from the Texas Parks and Wildlife Department Fish Record and Award website. (Posted on August 2, 2018)

SPECIES	LBS.	INCHES	DATE	METHOD
REMORA	4.00	28.25	29-OCT-17	S RR A
CATFISH, HARDHEAD	1.69	16.75	17-OCT-14	S RR FF A
JACK, ALMACO	3.25	19.50	01-JAN-14	S RR FF A
MACKEREL, KING	30.40	51.00	13-NOV-16	S RR FF A
REMORA	4.00	28.25	29-OCT-17	S RR FF A
SNAPPER, RED	12.69	29.25	12-OCT-14	S RR FF A
SNAPPER, VERMILION	3.00	19.75	13-NOV-16	S RR FF A
TRIGGERFISH, GRAY	2.30	17.50	17-OCT-14	S RR FF A
COBIA		40.25	30-OCT-17	S CR RR A
JACK, CREVALLE		41.50	15-OCT-10	S CR RR A
MACKEREL, KING		43.00	24-FEB-13	S CR RR N
TUNNY, LITTLE		26.00	15-OCT-10	S CR RR A
COBIA		40.25	30-OCT-17	S CR FF A
SNAPPER, RED		25.25	15-JUN-13	S CR FF A
TUNNY, LITTLE		26.00	15-OCT-10	S CR FF A
BONNETHEAD	7.60	40.00	11-OCT-16	S OM PL N
CATFISH, GAFFTOPSAIL	3.57	21.25	03-FEB-13	S OM PL N
CATFISH, HARDHEAD	1.19	14.75	13-OCT-14	S OM PL N
DRUM, RED	22.80	40.00	10-OCT-16	S OM PL N
LADYFISH	1.31	20.00	14-OCT-11	S OM PL A
MACKEREL, SPANISH	4.11	23.75	11-OCT-11	S OM PL A
PINFISH	0.51	10.25	30-JUN-12	S OM PL N
REMORA	2.70	26.25	01-DEC-12	S OM HL N
SEATROUT, SAND	1.13	15.25	23-SEP-12	S OM PL N
SEATROUT, SPOTTED	1.01	15.25	14-OCT-14	S OM PL N
SHARK, ATL. SHARPNOSE	9.20	39.50	05-JUL-12	S OM HL N

- TABLE 1 -

S = Saltwater **F** = Freshwater **FP** = Freshwater Private
RR = Rod & Reel **HL** = Handline **CR** = Catch & Release
FF = Fly Fishing **OM** = Other Methods **BA** = Bow & Arrow
A = Artificial Bait **PL** = Pole & Line No Reel (Plnor)

SPECIES	LBS.	INCHES	DATE	METHOD
SHARK, BLACKTIP	9.81	32.00	10-OCT-16	S OM PL N
SHARK, SPINNER	7.10	0.00	09-OCT-16	S OM PL N
SHARKSUCKER	2.90	26.25	13-NOV-16	S OM HL N
STINGRAY, ATLANTIC	7.49	35.00	28-DEC-15	S OM PL N
STINGRAY, BLUNTNOSE	5.33	31.00	29-MAY-15	S OM PL N
TOADFISH, GULF	0.66	10.00	08-OCT-11	S OM HL N
TILAPIA, HYBRID	4.15	18.00	28-SEP-17	F RR N
BUFFALO, BLACK		36.25	18-DEC-16	F CR RR N
CARP, COMMON		34.25	03-AUG-13	F CR FF A
BASS, ALABAMA	0.67	12.50	02-DEC-17	F OM PL N
BASS, HYBRID STRIPED	7.60	25.00	29-DEC-11	F OM PL A
BASS, LARGEMOUTH	8.01	24.50	01-JUL-18	F OM PL N
BASS, SMALLMOUTH	2.46	16.50	26-JUN-14	F OM PL N
BASS, STRIPED	10.75	30.50	30-MAY-17	F OM PL N
BASS, WHITE X YELLOW	0.73	10.50	11-JUN-13	F OM PL A
BUFFALO, BLACK	17.50	30.50	13-AUG-16	F OM PL N
TILAPIA, BLUE	4.55	17.25	08-JUN-14	F OM PL N
TILAPIA, HYBRID	3.23	14.00	21-MAY-16	F OM PL N
TROUT, RAINBOW	4.75	22.50	13-DEC-14	F OM PL N
CARP, COMMON	20.80	31.25	18-JUN-18	FP RR FF A
TILAPIA, BLUE	3.07	15.75	18-AUG-17	FP RR FF A
TILAPIA, HYBRID	2.18	15.00	18-AUG-17	FP RR FF A
DRUM, FRESHWATER	3.28	21.00	11-JUN-18	FP BA
TILAPIA, BLUE	2.19	15.50	18-AUG-17	FP BA
TILAPIA, HYBRID	3.17	16.00	14-AUG-17	FP BA

Karen Osborn is holding a 39-inch blue catfish resulting in the Lake Lewisville catch and release waterbody record.

In some ways, my 2.9-pound sharksucker state record on a handline gives me more satisfaction than my 30.4-pound state record king mackerel on a fly rod. Although both fish were caught on the same day, the sharksucker was especially exciting because the fish was observed in the water. My throw was made directly to the fish with just a spool of line and a hook. My preparation of carrying a handline resulted in landing the sharksucker state record.

- WATERBODY RECORDS -

The wind bounced the boat up and down as we anchored near a peninsula on Lake Lewisville in Texas. Karen informed our guide that her goal was to catch a blue catfish that would result in a big fish award and count as one of the five big fish awards she needed to achieve her freshwater elite angler award. We had already landed several catfish including my 37-inch blue catfish qualifying for a big fish award, so Karen knew there were big blue catfish in the area as she threw out her line and waited in anticipation.

With only a few hours left to fish, one of Karen's poles bent over hard. She removed the rod from the holder, and the battle was on. It was obvious from the beginning that this was a big fish. The guide's rod butt was longer than Karen normally uses, and she was struggling to get the rod in position to gain leverage on the fish. The fish was not helping as it rolled, swam under the boat, and pulled line from the reel. She worked the fish slowly and recovered line on the reel. She coaxed the fish to the boat, and the captain netted the blue catfish and placed it on a measuring board. The fish was 39 inches long and weighed 28.75 pounds. The fish was a new catch and release waterbody record for the lake and qualified for the big fish award Karen needed toward her freshwater elite angler award qualification.

Few states maintain waterbody records for lakes and rivers, but if you fish in one of these states, the chance of catching a record increases. Waterbody records are frequently dominated by local anglers and can be broken into different categories including rod and reel, catch and release, fly fishing, and bowfishing. It is common for a single angler to hold over 50 percent of the species records for a waterbody in a specific category. Always check the availability of local waterbody records where you are fishing, so you do not pass up the chance to document a record. Some states contain annual records for a waterbody, and every year they reset the data giving you additional opportunities to receive a new record.

- WEIGHT RECORDS -

After researching the nearby freshwater lakes, we determined the best way for Karen to add to her freshwater elite angler award was to catch a hybrid striped bass, so we booked a fishing trip. The guide looked at me with curiosity when he realized my rod did not contain a reel, and he became concerned once he realized we had two goals for the trip. The first was for Karen to achieve a big fish award toward her freshwater elite angler award qualification, and the second was to set a state record using my pole and line no reel (Plnor) technique. I think the guide was expecting normal anglers on this trip.

Karen was enjoying a great day of fishing and landed over ten white bass and hybrid striped bass when my first fish hooked-up. It was a small hybrid striped bass, and by utilizing the Plnor method, the fish would qualify as a state record in the other methods category. The fish was weighed, and the appropriate pictures were taken before returning the potential state record fish to the water.

Toward the end of the trip, a big fish hit my lure. Slight pressure on the line kept it tight as the line slid through my fingers. The spool of line clanked loudly in the five-gallon bucket at my feet as the line came rapidly off the spool and swiftly out of the bucket. The fish finally stopped running, and the process of stripping the fish back to the boat began. After steady progress, the fish finally surfaced and was netted. We laid the hybrid striped bass on a measuring board, and it barely reached the 25-inch mark to qualify as a big fish. The fish was placed on a scale. At 7.6 pounds the hybrid striped bass (whiterock bass) was later certified as the new Texas state record in the other methods category for pole and line fishing without a reel.

The fish would also be certified as the FFHF catch and release world record in division 3. The catch easily exceeded the weight of my state record fish caught earlier in the day. Although we were originally after a record fish based on length, I ended the trip with both a weight record and a length record catch. Karen never caught the 25-inch hybrid striped bass required for her big fish award, so we were already planning another trip.

Weight records are the most common method of documenting record fish. Almost all states maintain weight records for rod and reel fishing. Some states separate weight records into other fishing techniques, such as fly fishing. This substantially improves an angler's chance to achieve a record.

The biggest obstacle when documenting a weight record is to find a certified scale. Review the scales section to learn how to overcome this obstacle, and keep in mind that a fish's weight is dependent on the species and condition. A short fish may actually weigh more than a longer fish of the same species, so do not eliminate your chances at a record by deciding not to weigh your fish because it is shorter than the record on the books. A world record fish may be small in size. To qualify for an IGFA or FFHF world record, a fish must weigh a minimum of one pound. States have different qualifications, and for some species, a state record fish may only weigh a few ounces.

- CATCH AND RELEASE RECORDS -

Gulls were actively hitting the water in several locations. A small school of striped mullet sped by the boat to avoid marauding predators. A long cast to the edge of the birds caused the fly line to straighten as it hit the water. With one strip the line quickly tightened. The hook embedded in a fish and a huge ladyfish rocketed from the water throwing the fly. When the fly returned to the water, another ladyfish immediately picked it up, but this time the hook dug in deep. The fight was on. The fish jumped again and again before coming to the net. It was easy to see how the fish had acquired the local name skipjack. Removing the hook, measurements and pictures were taken. We released the 21-inch fish to fight another day. The catch resulted in a catch and release big fish award certificate.

Catch and release fishing has gained popularity over the last few decades increasing the quantity and quality of fish available. Because of the desire of many anglers to release fish, several states have added a catch and release category to their record programs.

World records were originally documented by weight. Both the IGFA and FFHF joined the catch and release craze by adding world record catch and release categories for several species. The FFHF added a catch and release program in 1993. In 2011, the IGFA added a catch and release program for world record categories. Although weight records have been around for decades, there are still hundreds of new world records replaced each year for fish based on weight. Since catch and release records have been added, anglers have new opportunities to receive a fishing world record.

Catch and release records are the easiest to document since they are based on length and do not require a certified scale. Be sure to follow all the rules when measuring your record since measurement methods vary between states and regions. Collect data quickly when working with catch and release fish. This is especially true for pelagic species like yellowfin or blackfin tuna. These fish and other open water pelagic species die rapidly if water is not moving over their gills.

Recording data for catch and release species is best accomplished through a team effort. There should be a coordinated plan in place to get all the pictures and information needed to record your record so you can make a quick release. A measuring board should be in place and a camera ready when a fish is removed from the water. The fish should be laid on a measuring board and pictures should be taken rapidly. The angler should take pictures with the fish including any pictures needed to identify its species. The fish should be returned to the water as soon as possible. With a good team, this can be done in less than a minute similar to a NASCAR pit-stop. Speed will protect the fish and get everyone fishing again for another record. Removing a fish from the water before you are ready to document a catch may cause the fish to die, and you will lose your catch and release record.

RECORDS AND RECOGNITION | 65

Catch and release records are easy to document since you do not need to weigh a fish. Barry Osborn released this 34-inch Squaw Creek Reservoir catch and release waterbody record common carp to be caught another day.

Delay celebrations until after a fish is released. A witness should observe the release to make sure the fish swims away unharmed. A fish sinking to the bottom or floating upside down on the surface does not count as a successful release.

Catch and release fishing is one of the most satisfying ways to fish and with the addition of new catch and release programs it can be very rewarding from a record standpoint. If you have your own certified scales, catch and release fishing may be practiced in conjunction with weight records by weighing and releasing fish.

- CERTIFICATES AND TROPHIES -

My two-year-old daughter Laura stood by the upland pond holding her Zebco reel on a short modified rod. The float was motionless for a few minutes until it began to move slightly. Finally, bobbing up and down frantically the float disappeared under the water. Laura began to reel as she was instructed. She continued turning the handle as she walked backward pulling the green sunfish onto the bank. She had landed her first fish by herself with a rod and reel. Today Laura fishes with me on a regular basis, but she does not remember this catch. A first fish award certificate could have been acquired from the state fish and wildlife department to memorialize the event, but my lack of knowledge about the rewards program allowed the documentation for this historic moment to be lost.

There are a variety of ways to achieve fishing recognition. One of my favorites is the first fish award. Many states and organizations issue a certificate for an angler's first fish. This certificate will last a lifetime and is the start of wonderful days on the water for an excited young angler. The satisfaction and thrill of this award may not be fully realized until adulthood when the angler finds the award tucked away in an old family album and shares it with future generations.

Certificates are a good way to award an angler that catches a unique or hard fighting fish that does not reach record status. Some states provide recognition certificates for anglers whose fish does not make the record books. The IGFA will issue a freshwater or saltwater catch certificate for a fee. These are nice certificates and look great framed and put on the wall. Other organizations provide certificates for specific species or outstanding catches. A certificate like this may be an excellent gift for a family member or friend. Documenting these achievements enhances the thrill and camaraderie of fishing as anglers look back on their fishing memories and share their experiences.

Trophies are another way to provide recognition for an angler. A trophy containing a fish sculpture can be presented to an angler under a variety of conditions. Fishing trophies are often attractive and generate discussions of fishing adventures for years to come. Many private organizations provide catch certificates and trophies for their members in varying categories. Trophies are usually provided at junior angler tournament events throughout the United States. The options for acquiring a certificate or trophy are endless.

- BRAGGING RIGHTS -

It was mid-week during our annual October fishing trip to the Texas coast. Several of my co-workers were on the trip, and the weather was spectacular with low winds and clear water. Today my boat contained Jim and Steve. My 21-foot Kenner center console boat was drifting slowly over the shallow flats of the bay. My gold spoon was cast many times into the open areas between the submerged grass beds. Suddenly, the calm drift was interrupted by Jim's call, "Fish on!" Steve quickly followed suit with the call, "Me too!" Having two fish on while drifting is usually not a problem since spotted seatrout and red drum usually run in one direction as you drift toward the fish. In this case, Jim's fish went away from the boat while Steve's fish made a lightning-fast run in the opposite direction. I reeled in my line to get out of the way and experienced a great deal of satisfaction as I enjoyed the double hook-up on my boat.

Both anglers were challenged by their fish. We were floating towards Jim's fish, and Steve's fish was still taking line in short bursts. It appeared Steve had a really big red drum on his line. Normally the engine would be started to pursue the fish. In this case, we would have to sacrifice one fish to save the other. While weighing my options, Steve's fish made a crazy run ripping line off the reel. Walking to the back of the boat to survey the situation Steve turned and looked at me with a worried expression.

Looking at Steve's reel, the spool was visible through the few wraps of line. A glance at Jim revealed he was making good headway, but he was still fighting his fish. Looking back at Steve I asked, "Are you going to get off the boat?" and he replied, "I'm thinking about it." We were drifting in less than two feet of water so stepping off the boat was an option. Getting off the boat with a fish on can be a tricky maneuver and may not assist in regaining line. Fortunately, Jim helped the situation by calling out, "I'm in!" as he lifted a humongous inshore lizardfish over the side. We would have been sick if we had lost Steve's red drum over an inshore lizardfish, but there was no way to know what Jim was fighting.

Returning my attention back to Steve, we were all excited about his fish. Steve's fish turned toward the boat, and he regained some line. The fish then began another lightning run. This time it was headed toward the front of the boat. Steve struggled to move forward while trying to retrieve his line fast enough to remove the slack that was quickly developing. The excitement was building as the fish forced Steve to run around the boat two more times.

We all knew this was a huge record fish. A few more runs and reaching over the gunnel the net engulfed the stocky medium sized 24-inch red drum instead of the 40-inch red drum we were expecting. Steve was worn out from the fight and looked at me as he stated, "Well it's not the size of the dog in the fight, but the size of the fight in the dog that matters."

Steve has caught much larger red drum, and this fish was not big enough to make the official record books, but recognition is not always recorded. The fish and the stellar fight will always be remembered. Twenty years later you can hear Steve recalling that day as he visits with a new generation of anglers. Anytime we hear about "the size of the dog in the fight" we both drift back to that day on the water when the cares of the world just did not matter.

Although not every fish will result in a record, many fish deserve bragging rights. Barry Osborn and Ken Laterza filled the freezer with Ken's large, delicious blacktip shark.

Enjoy every moment you have fishing, they can stay with you for a lifetime. There are fish fights you will remember where the only recognition you receive is the satisfaction of a treasured moment.

Your attitude toward another angler is more important than pursuing a record. One day an angler on my boat was not catching any fish, while the other members of the group were slaying crevalle jack, Spanish mackerel, and small blacktip sharks. The deprived fisherman was frustrated but finally hooked a nice spinner shark that he fought for about 20 minutes. The fish jumped high in the air multiple times and gave a spectacular fight.

During the spinner shark's final leap beside the boat, the steel leader wrapped around the shark's body and pulled the monofilament toward its tail. When the fish hit the water, the line snapped. Another fish was lost, but for the rest of the day, I talked about the fisherman's fantastic spinner shark hook-up. It was truly an inspiring fight with a great fish. That evening I smiled as he told his spouse about the tale of the hook-up and the fight with the magnificent fish. Over the years, he has repeated this story with pride even though he never landed the fish. Always help others appreciate the wonderful opportunities we have in our sport. Sometimes bragging rights are better than a certificate, trophy, or getting your name in the record books.

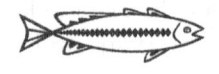

4

UNCONVENTIONAL METHODS

- RULES AND REGULATIONS -

The boat moved back and forth gently in two-foot seas as the rope tied to the offshore oil rig tightened in the wind. It was a fantastic day of fishing. We landed numerous fish including a nice 46-inch cobia. The chum was working well, and the bait only sank a few yards before being consumed by a fish. Looking over the gunnel, we saw red shapes below the boat. We had landed vermilion snapper at this rig in the past, and it appeared we had lured some near the surface with chum. My fly rod with 16-pound tippet and eight weight sinking line was in the boat, so for extra fun, the fly rod came out.

Several false casts worked the line off the fly reel until a long cast was made toward the chum. After several seconds of slowly stripping the line, the fly moved through the chum. Suddenly the line headed under the boat toward the rig. As the line cleared the corner of the boat, I lifted the rod and embedded the hook in the fish. Line peeled off the reel, and the fish was well into the backing before slowing down. This was not a vermilion snapper. The fish dove deep and went into the rig. Moving to the bow of the boat my goal was to fight the fish up and down to keep it out of the rig supports. It was a long fight. Finally, the fish tired and swam to the surface where we netted it and lifted it over the gunnel of the boat. It was a nice red snapper that weighed over 20 pounds. The red snapper exceeded the current

IGFA world record on 16-pound tippet by several pounds. A potential tippet class world record fish was lying on my boat deck. My heart sank when I realized red snapper season was closed. There was no way around this fact to document the record. Even with certified scales, the IGFA requires fish to be weighed on land, and legally this fish could not be retained. The hook was removed from the red snapper, and the fish was gently pulled back and forth through the water until it was revived. The potential world record fish swam away.

Most record organizations indicate that a record fish must be caught within existing state or federal regulations. Unfortunately, in today's world, regulations are complicated, and many situations fall within a gray area. Misinformed anglers can lose records. In addition, if they do not comply with existing regulations, they may face the consequences of unwanted legal action. Changes occur regularly in fishing rules, and many fish are now listed as protected species. You do not want to turn in a record submittal form to an enforcement agency for a fish that was illegally caught.

Thoroughly understanding the rules for unconventional fishing methods can result in numerous fishing records depending on where you fish. States vary concerning fishing record regulations when using unconventional methods. Unfortunately, many states do not recognize these methods in their record programs. Some states and organizations lump these methods together while others separate certain methods, such as bowfishing or ice fishing, into distinct record categories. Through creativity, you can utilize different methods to achieve records. Some of the methods reviewed in this chapter are only allowed in limited circumstances or for non-game fish. If you harvest a fish unlawfully, your record will not count and could result in the loss of all your previous records as well as potential fines.

As you review the unconventional methods of fishing, remember that fishing with one method can exclude the possibility of a fishing record in a different category. All of the methods in this section, except fly fishing, will eliminate the possibility of achieving an IGFA world record since IGFA records require a rod and reel. Beyond rod and reel fishing, these unconventional methods can result in FFHF world records for fly fishing, Plnor fishing, or ice fishing. Many unconventional methods have been modified for ice fishing.

If your state does not allow unconventional methods in their records program, there is an opportunity to work with your fish and wildlife department to incorporate a program with unconventional methods. Catch and release programs were adopted by many states within the last decade and expanding a state's record program to include unconventional methods may be possible. If a new unconventional method category is added to your state's program, then several new records will become available.

The desire to use unconventional methods is a personal preference. When fishing with other methods, there are often strange looks and questions from bystanders concerning the method being applied. You can try these methods for the fun of it or for a new challenge. Some unconventional methods require skill and have a learning curve. For me, fishing with unconventional methods is gratifying. When I discuss catching a state record Atlantic sharpnose shark on a handline it generates interesting conversation. You can justify your own reasons to use the following methods but always consider safety first.

- FISHING BY HAND -

Red snapper were feeding heavily, and we had nearly reached our allotted bag limit. My friend Ken was in the process of landing another big red snapper. While throwing pieces of chum over the gunnel, a grayish brown fish swam out from under the boat grabbing several pieces of chum. The fish eagerly consumed a squid head. It was a large remora, and he was hungry and aggressive. To persuade the fish to move closer, I dangled a piece of squid just below the surface of the water. The remora was leery at first but finally took the squid from my hand. After more pieces of squid were consumed by the fish, we were good friends. Eventually, the remora waited at the surface until more squid were provided. Ken looked over and said, "What are you doing?" and I replied, "I am feeding my friend." Ken walked over to take a look, and the fish took another squid from my hand. As the next piece of squid was lowered into the water, the remora swam over again. Suddenly, Ken reached down and grabbed the fish by the tail and jerked it from the water. He looked at the fish and said, "I got you, you little bait stealer." He dropped the fish back over the side, and it shot off never to be seen again…so much for friendship.

Fishing by hand is one of the oldest fishing methods. There are few circumstances where you can catch a free-swimming fish by hand. Interestingly this method of fishing is illegal in many states, especially for game fish. Always check the regulations before you fish by hand.

The best-known method of hand fishing is for freshwater catfish often called noodling. The popularity of this sport has increased interest in hand fishing throughout the United States. Channel catfish, flathead catfish, and blue catfish can be taken by hand in some states. If you are interested in this type of fishing method, guides are available on the internet. Fishing by hand is often included in the unrestricted methods category or in the other methods category for fishing records. Therefore it may be difficult to obtain a record catfish when noodling since you are competing for a record that may be documented using various other methods including trotlines. Fishing opportunities are limited in saltwater for catching a fish by hand, but in areas where it is legal you can definitely receive bragging rights.

- NETS -

The deep blue water surrounding the oil rig was an excellent habitat for several species of fish and resulted in a wonderful day of family fishing excitement. Karen and our young daughters, Laura and Cindy, were laughing, talking, and catching fish. During the day we landed red snapper, gray snapper, king mackerel, dolphin, cobia, and numerous other species. The winds were calm, the seas were low, and we only had a few fish left to complete our red snapper limit before we were planning to head back to port. Weed patches were floating by our boat with small gray triggerfish feeding from them.

My youngest daughter Cindy decided to take a break from fishing. She grabbed a landing net and indicated she was going to catch a gray triggerfish. The clear water would make it difficult to capture a fish, and my response to her included my lack of faith in her ability to net one. My daughter is a high achiever, and my lack of encouragement fueled her fire to net a fish. She started by slapping the net at the fish with no success. Then she tried sneaking up on the fish with the same results. Since she was enjoying herself, I continued red snapper fishing. After several minutes Cindy proclaimed, "Gotcha!" from the bow of the boat. Looking at my sweet young daughter, she was smiling from ear to ear while holding up two gray triggerfish in her net.

Nets have been used for fishing throughout recorded history, and net fishing encompasses a wide variety of fishing techniques. Fishing nets include but are not limited to cast nets, gill nets, dip nets, seines, trawls, and umbrella nets. Every state regulates the use of nets for fishing. These regulations vary greatly and are often confusing. For example, in Texas, a cast net can be used to take non-game fish in both saltwater and freshwater, but in saltwater, the netted fish may be taken for bait purposes only. In Texas, nets were included in the other methods category for setting records, but a change to their program currently excludes nets as a method for catching record fish.

Rules are often unclear about the use of nets for setting records. If a state contains unconventional methods and nets are not excluded as a legal fishing method, you may be able to set records utilizing a net. Contact your state fisheries department to determine if fishing with a net can result in a record. Ultimately the decision to document a record is up to the certifying agency. Check online data frequently as regulations concerning legal methods may change.

- TROTLINES, SETLINES, JUGLINES -

As a youngster, I was fishing with Don, a family friend, from a small boat on the Trinity River in Texas. Only a few minutes had passed after we finished putting out three plastic gallon bottles as juglines. Eventually, the first jug started bouncing up and down. Then it took off straight up the river. This was a new fishing style for me, and I was intrigued as we started the engine and pursued the jug.

Check regulations when using unconventional methods. Cindy Osborn is featured with two legally netted free-swimming gray triggerfish.

Years later while watching the movie Jaws, my thoughts wandered back to memories of the jug moving up the river as water was forced to either side of it as the bottle occasionally disappeared beneath the surface. Finally, the jug stopped as we slowly approached it. While carefully lifting the jug, Don tied the jug leader line to a large fishing rod and delicately removed it. He tightened the line on the reel and slowly took up the slack.

The reel screamed as the fish felt the resistance and swam up the river. The drag was heavy, and the small boat was being pulled by the powerful fish. The struggle was intense, but Don finally pulled the small five-foot alligator gar to the boat. The fish was not a record, but it was the largest freshwater fish I had ever seen. Don unhooked the fish and watched as it swam away proclaiming, "That was fun! Now, let's go get another one!"

Trotlines, setlines, and juglines are defined as unrestricted or other methods for legal fishing in several states. Fish caught using these methods may count as records depending on the state's regulations. Nomenclature of fishing methods varies greatly between states.

Typically a trotline is defined as a multiple line rig attached to a structure or buoy at both ends. Setlines or throwlines are lines tied to a permanent structure at one end. Juglines contain a floating device and are usually allowed to float freely. Tip-ups are sophisticated modified setlines for ice fishing.

If records for unconventional methods are allowed many anglers believe that trotlines, setlines, and juglines give an angler an unfair advantage for obtaining records. Most state fish and wildlife departments separate these fishing techniques from traditional rod and reel records. Monstrous catfish weighing more than 100 pounds and alligator gar weighing more than 300 pounds have been caught with trotlines, setlines, and juglines.

Since regulations vary, be careful when using these methods. Many states have kept records using these fishing methods for years, and therefore some of the records may be difficult to replace. The FFHF maintains records for ice fishing, and you can achieve a world record for ice fishing using a tip-up or other varied legal device.

For some species, records in unconventional method categories are vacant and readily available. For example, Utah has a separate state record category for setline fishing, but only a few state record entries have been documented when using a setline. If you want a quick state record, then acquire a setline permit in Utah and start fishing.

- HAND SPEARS AND SPEARGUNS -

It was a bright night in David's boat as the full moon reflected across the relatively calm waters. We were teenagers and were traveling down to the Lower Laguna Madre near the Mexican border to fish. The handheld spotlights were tied to the boat rail. The lights illuminated the bottom of the bay as we drifted over the shallow water.

We were floating over a mosaic of dark grass and light sandy patches looking for the oval outline of a southern flounder. David let me borrow his Hawaiian sling. The Hawaiian sling was in my hand ready for a shot as we slowly drifted over the flats. We had already speared several nice southern flounder when a sandy spot appeared containing the dark outline of a large fish.

The spear made a slight popping noise as it entered the water. Instead of a delicious potential southern flounder meal, the water erupted with the flinging tail and barb of a big southern stingray. The fish tried to get away and nearly pulled me off the boat. I held onto the spear as the southern stingray began wildly flapping and spinning in the water. Finally, it came loose and swam away. Lifting the spear into the boat revealed that not only was the southern stingray gone, but the three-pronged spearhead was also missing. The southern stingray had spun long enough to unscrew the spearhead from the Hawaiian sling. David looked at me and with a smirk and said, "You owe me twenty bucks." It's great to have friends.

Spearfishing encompasses a wide variety of fishing methods from simple gigging to very expensive spearguns. Regulations governing spearfishing vary, and you should consult your state fish and wildlife department to determine if fish can be legally harvested with a spear or speargun. Typically spearfishing is only legal for non-game fish.

Spearfishing is more common in saltwater but can also occur in freshwater. Spearfishing records will usually fall within other methods or unrestricted non-rod and reel categories. Fish taken with a speargun can weigh several hundred pounds. The Texas state record for a goliath grouper harvested with a speargun is 660 pounds from 1975. Since the goliath grouper is now protected, this record will likely remain as the unrestricted state record in this category.

Although it may be challenging to compete with other anglers who are utilizing unrestricted fishing techniques, freshwater and saltwater opportunities for records are still available. A few fish species speared in freshwater include common carp, smallmouth buffalo, and gar species. In saltwater, a larger variety of fish species are harvested with a speargun including crevalle jack, great barracuda, and southern flounder. Due to the vast opportunities available, vacant categories may exist. If you try spearfishing, have fun and stay safe since this method can be extremely dangerous.

- BOWFISHING -

A few days had passed since fourteen inches of rain fell in the watershed. The water was muddy, and the flood waters were receding across the Bermuda grass pasture into the pecan bottom as the water flowed toward the river. Dorsal fins of large smallmouth buffalo protruded from the water as the fish crossed a flooded spot on the road trying to reach the river. My excitement built as I hurried to my truck to retrieve my bow. I returned to the water's edge and waited patiently for a chance to shoot a fish.

A slight movement in the water prompted me to draw my Browning compound bow. The white fiberglass arrow was tied to 40-pound monofilament line attached to a Zebco 888 reel mounted on the front of the bow. The smallmouth buffalo rose slightly to clear a berm as the arrow intercepted the fish. The fish then shot across the current swiftly pulling line from the reel. I placed the bow under my arm to reel in the fish. The fight was easy since the arrow entered a vital area of the fish's body. After a few minutes, it was pulled onto

80 | THE ART OF FISHING FOR RECORDS

The challenging sport of bowfishing can result in records. In the mid-1980s, Barry Osborn harvested two smallmouth buffalo.

the road. Although it was not a record, it was a nice 36-inch smallmouth buffalo. Another swirl in the water caught my attention, so I quickly retrieved my arrow to prepare for the next shot.

Bowfishing is an excellent way to achieve a record. Many states have a separate category for bowfishing. Record opportunities are plentiful for some species since there are few bowfishing entries. Although this is true, several documented records include large fish and may require extra effort to replace. Some states combine bowfishing with non-rod and reel categories. Therefore you may be competing with other unconventional methods including spearguns, trotlines, and throwlines when trying to achieve a bowfishing record.

Since 1990 the Bowfishing Association of America (BAA) has maintained bowfishing records throughout the United States. The BAA maintains and provides certificates for both state and world bowfishing records giving an enthusiast of this method a centralized location for bowfishing record information. Since applications to the BAA may differ from applications to a state fish and wildlife department, state records posted by the BAA are often not the same records as those posted by individual states. This provides additional opportunities to achieve a bowfishing record. Be sure to check multiple record organizations to receive additional recognition. BAA world record certificates are provided for the largest specimen of a fish species harvested with a bow and arrow. The world and state bowfishing records are based on weight. BAA record requirements can be located online at bowfishingassociation.com.

Where it is legal, saltwater fishing provides unique angling opportunities with a bow and arrow. Few anglers utilize this method while fishing in saltwater. A wide variety of fish species are available both in the bay and offshore, and many saltwater bowfishing records are vacant. Bowfishing in saltwater provides an excellent avenue for an eager angler to capitalize on potential records.

Bowfishing is an invigorating and adventurous way to fish. It takes time and practice to master the art, but once you acquire the knowledge to be successful, bowfishing can be enjoyed for a lifetime. As you implement this unconventional method, be sure to carefully review bowfishing regulations to avoid harvesting illegal fish species. Regulations differ between states and cities, so make sure it is legal to possess and use a bow in an area where you intend to fish.

- HANDLINE FISHING -

My wife Karen was eager to get out of the house for a fun fishing trip. We completed our seven-hour drive to the Texas coast and checked into our condominium. We decided to catch pinfish for bait, so we drove over to an easy access point in the harbor. My anticipation was building while reaching for the five-gallon bucket containing the spool of Magibraid line tied to an old fly line with a six-foot leader, a weight, a Mustad UltraPoint hook, and a piece of squid. Although we were there to catch bait, using the unconventional fishing method of a handline provided an exceptional chance for a potential record. Handline fishing falls within the other methods category in Texas.

Karen was using her favorite Zebco 888 reel on a Shakespeare rod, and she caught a pinfish when there was a tug on the end of my line. A slight pop of the line followed, and a fish was on. The line was slowly stripped into a bucket while bringing the fish toward the shore. The fight was uneventful. After a few swirls and flips, the gulf toadfish was lifted from the water. The state and waterbody record lists for the bay had been printed the night before, and the other methods category state record list revealed a vacant category for a gulf toadfish. Filling a five-gallon bucket with water, the gulf toadfish was dropped into the bucket to keep it alive for pictures, weighing, and measurements. The fish was ten inches long and weighed 0.66 pounds. After taking the required pictures, the fish was released, and the potential new state record swam away. The paperwork was submitted to the Texas Parks and Wildlife Department, and my unrestricted state record certificate was received a few weeks later.

The term handline fishing covers a wide variety of fishing styles and equipment. It is one of the oldest recorded methods of fishing and is still widely used in many countries and commonly used throughout the United States. Handline fishing is a simple, inexpensive method to catch fish. It can be as easy as tying a line to a water bottle or purchasing a commercial handline spool or device.

Fishing with a handline can be implemented in both freshwater and saltwater. Landing a fish over 30 inches in length using a handline is exciting. Handline fishing requires practice due to the delicate balance of setting the hook, allowing a fish to run, preventing burns on your hands, and avoiding breaking the line.

Caution must be exercised while handline fishing. Use of braided line is not recommended. Accidentally wrapping a line around a finger could result in a permanent injury if a big fish takes your bait. Backing tied to a fly line with a long leader is great for handline fishing. Fly line is much easier and safer for your hands than monofilament line. Monofilament line will burn your hands more rapidly than a fly line in most situations. Fly line has adequate strength for many fish species. Parachute cord is another great option for really large fish, but be very cautious when fighting a fish with parachute cord of heavy breaking strength. Broken fingers or life-threatening situations can occur if you become tangled in the line.

Regulations governing handline fishing vary widely between states. Several states do not specifically address handline fishing, and this method may fall in a separate category. Depending on the interpretation of a state's regulations, handline fishing for some species may be illegal since it does not fall within the legally required pole and line fishing method category. Always review all state fish and wildlife department regulations before handline fishing especially if you intend to harvest game fish.

- CANE POLE AND TENKARA -

The year was 1969. My young hands reached into a metal coffee can for an earthworm that my grandfather "Buster" had dug up with me that morning. It was a warm Oklahoma summer day. Buster handed me an old cane pole and slid a squirming earthworm on a hook tied to a heavy black nylon line. A cork float was attached to the line. Lowering the cane pole, the earthworm entered the water under an overhanging black willow tree. The float began to slowly move then disappeared under the water. Lifting the cane pole from the water revealed a large bluegill. As the fish reached the bank, my eyes turned toward my grandfather. From the look on his face, you would have thought my fish was a grander blue marlin. He exclaimed, "That's a good one!" while grabbing the fish and placing it on my stringer. We caught so many bluegills that day we had trouble carrying them all back to the pickup. Not only were we fishing for fun, but we were fishing to catch enough food for a good meal. As we walked back up the cow path, my grandfather bragged about how my fishing efforts helped put food on the table for our family. Although there were no official records achieved that day, the recognition my grandfather gave me has stayed with me throughout my life and wildlife career.

Fishing with a natural cane pole is one of the oldest forms of fishing in the United States. Many garages still contain pieces of old cane poles that belonged to a distant relative and some people still fish with natural homemade cane poles today. Modern "cane poles" are often made of fiberglass, graphite, or other new materials and are used for a variety of species including crappie. Fish including sunfish and crappie are well suited to pursue with a cane pole.

When considering records, states vary in how they view fishing with this method since a cane pole consists of a line attached to a rod without a reel. Some states have record programs that only allow rod and reel fishing, and this category does not include cane pole fishing. In these states, cane pole fishing may fall within other methods or unrestricted categories. Other states define their records as rod and reel records, and their definition of this category encompasses pole and line fishing even if a reel is not included.

Tenkara is a method of fly fishing from Japan similar to cane pole fishing with aspects of fly fishing without a reel. Tenkara fishing has been used in other countries for years but has recently become popular in the United States. There are tenkara rods sold specifically for this fishing technique. Tenkara fishing has the same limitation as cane pole fishing since a limited amount of line can be attached directly to a rod. Records for tenkara fishing are similar to the pole and line category and may be included under the rod and reel record category or may fall within other methods or unrestricted record categories depending on the state. A fish caught with either a cane pole or a tenkara pole may result in an FFHF world record for pole and line fishing without a reel.

- PLNOR FISHING -

Although we planned a day of offshore fishing the seas were high, so we booked a trip on a boat out of Dolphin Docks in Port Aransas, Texas for an afternoon of bay fishing. Captain Tim indicated they were catching big red drum at the north jetty during the afternoon, so we were optimistic. It was a cool October morning. There were only 11 people booked on the boat, and there was plenty of room for fishing. Armed with this information my rod and reel setup was replaced with my saltwater Plnor (pole and line no reel) fishing equipment. Plnor fishing often attracts attention from other anglers since a rod does not possess a reel.

On this trip, there were a few skeptics in the group. One angler said, "I am going to land a big red drum measuring over 30 inches, and nobody can land a fish that size without a reel." Fishing was fantastic that afternoon and watching several anglers land nice red drum up to 36 inches made me wonder when it would be my turn.

Even my wife was having success. She landed a beautiful 37-inch red drum that counted toward her saltwater elite angler award. Karen caught her fish on a small bass rod and reel with 12-pound test line that Captain Tim had put out hoping for Spanish mackerel. When Karen's fish hit, the rod bent over nearly past the handle. She grabbed the rod, and it was a long fight, but she skillfully reeled in the fish.

The trip was nearly over when something picked up my bait. Embedding the hook by hand can be tricky, so the line was slowly tightened to take up the slack before providing a quick jerk to dig in the hook. The hook set was hard, but the pressure was quickly released to keep from breaking the line. The fly line slid rapidly through my fingers, and then the backing started to run off the spool lying in the bucket at my feet. Finally, the fish stopped, and the work of stripping the fish back to the boat began. It would not be a one-way trip as the fish took line out several more times before giving it back again. This back and forth action went on for several minutes before gaining positive momentum on the fish. A scare came when I briefly missed the line on a hand transition allowing the fish to pull the line very close to the trim tab as it swam under the boat. The fish was finally netted and brought onboard. The beautiful 19.60-pound, 40.25-inch red drum qualified as an unrestricted Texas state record in the other methods category using the Plnor method.

Plnor fishing is a modified pole and line no reel technique that is more versatile than cane pole fishing since Plnor fishing allows you to select the amount of line you want to wind onto a spool. By refining the Plnor technique over the years, my tackle includes a rod and line on a spool that is only attached to the rod by threading the line through the rod guides.

In extreme cases, a glove and heavy parachute cord line are used. This technique is a mix of handline fishing, cane pole fishing, fly fishing, and conventional rod and reel fishing. The addition of fly fishing techniques added to the Plnor method has greatly increased the effectiveness of Plnor fishing, especially when using light lures.

You can Plnor fish using almost any fishing rod you have. Cut the line from your rod and remove the reel. Run the line from a spool through the rod guides and add whatever terminal tackle you normally use. The spool is often dropped inside a bucket to contain the line. If you decide to make a cast, pull line from the spool and place it on the ground next to the bucket, then cast your lure or bait. A weighted line can be lowered directly into the water to pull line off the spool when Plnor fishing from a boat or dock.

The bucket can be used to contain the stripped line while a fish is being fought. The line is stripped into the bucket or onto the deck and not rewound on the spool until after the process of fighting a fish concludes. My equipment includes several different rods and line weights for varying conditions. This technique will work with a casting rod, spinning rod, or a fly rod.

UNCONVENTIONAL METHODS | 87

Plnor fishing is an exciting way to fish. Fishing without a reel can result in bragging rights. This large 19.60-pound, 40.25-inch red drum was the unrestricted Texas state record caught using the Plnor method until it was replaced by a 22.8-pound red drum.

For my state record red drum, the rod was a 15-40 pound Bass Pro graphite series muskie rod. The line consisted of a six foot, 30-pound leader tied to a weight forward eight weight sinking (WF8S) fly line, connected to a 50-pound Magibraid backing wound onto a plastic spool. The spool was then placed into a bucket to contain it.

One of my favorite Plnor setups consists of a graphite nine-weight fly rod with a 20-pound Berkley Big Game leader tied to a WF9S clear fly line connected to a 50-pound Magibraid backing. This rig can be cast like a fly rod and has been effective on multiple occasions for both saltwater and freshwater species.

Like any unconventional technique, Plnor fishing is challenging. It is not recommended for anglers that have a tendency to become frustrated with tangled lines and missed fish. Use caution when fishing with this method. Monofilament line can easily cut you when you hook a big fish. Do not use braided fishing line when Plnor fishing. Tangles are often a problem, and more than one of my rods has been destroyed when a big fish tried to pull a tangled wad of the line through the rod guides. Casting can be difficult, but with practice, you can cover an area nearly as large as you do when using a conventional rod and reel with either bait or lures. You can easily cover a much larger area with this method compared to using a cane pole or tenkara. Backup spools of line are beneficial since a line can become tangled beyond recovery in the field.

You must always be diligent and aware concerning the location of your line. Although it is frustrating to cast a line after you realize you are standing on it, it is much more serious if you are trying to untangle a knot and a big fish takes your bait while you have the line wrapped around your fingers. Extra care should be taken if children are around. Besides tangling a line beyond repair, children could become wrapped in the line causing potential injury.

In some states, the Plnor method of fishing is included in the same category as fishing with a regular rod and reel. In other states, this technique results in an unconventional record category since a reel is not used. The downside when fishing with this technique is that it eliminates the chance of catching an IGFA world record

Almost any rod can be used for Plnor fishing. Small ice fishing rods, spinning rods, fly rods, casting rods, and offshore rods can be utilized. A fly line is often attached between the leader and backing to protect your hands. Parachute cord can be implemented to catch a big fish. The spool is independent of the rod and only attached to the rod by the line.

and possibly a state rod and reel weight record. However, the Plnor method is ideal for catching an FFHF world record, and it is one of the most exciting fishing methods in existence. Keeping one's hands on a line transfers every fish movement to the angler. The satisfaction of landing a big fish while viewing your tangled line running along the bank is exhilarating. You need to try it out for yourself.

- FLY FISHING -

As we passed the jetty and entered offshore waters, it appeared this was going to be a good morning for fishing. Bait balls were evident from a few yards off the tip of the jetty to the horizon. Pelicans and gulls filled the air. It was another stellar morning of fishing with my wife Karen and our friends Ken and Kim. Ken positioned his 24-foot Sea Pro boat upwind of a large bait ball and put the engine in neutral. He picked up a rod and cast a spoon toward the bait ball. He was immediately rewarded with a Spanish mackerel. As indicated previously, Ken loves to catch Spanish mackerel. To have a full appreciation of the fishing event, you have to envision an adult man running up and down his boat giggling while he throws Spanish mackerel everywhere on the deck so he can quickly get out another cast. We all enjoyed a pleasurable morning of filling the fish box.

After boating a few Spanish mackerel on a rod and reel, I removed my favorite fly rod from the rod holder in anticipation of catching a Spanish mackerel on a fly. The first cast sent my favorite shrimp fly near the edge of the bait ball. The plan was to let it sink for a few seconds and then begin to slowly retrieve it back toward the boat. One fish had a different plan. Swimming under a full head of steam, the fish grabbed the fly as soon as it landed in the water. Instinctively I set the hook, and the line tightened. Immediately all of the fly line was gone, and half of the backing was off the fly reel. This was not a Spanish mackerel. After a few minutes of fighting, the fish dove deep into the water and then the steady work of bringing it back up to the surface began. After about ten minutes, we could see color and identified the fish as a large little tunny.

UNCONVENTIONAL METHODS | 91

Many people equate fly fishing with species like rainbow trout. In fact, there are hundreds of fish species that can be caught while fly fishing. Barry Osborn's 30.4-pound king mackerel is a Texas fly fishing state record.

Karen watched as the fight went on and she examined the Gulf of Mexico fish record list. The state record catch and release category for little tunny was vacant, but the fish needed to be at least 22 inches long to qualify for a big fish award and catch and release state record. This fish was not the largest little tunny of my fishing career, but it was well over 22 inches long. If the fish could be landed for pictures and quick measurements, then released unharmed, the catch could qualify as a state catch and release record.

The fish was worn out when it reached the boat and Ken reached over the gunnel and grabbed its tail. He then quickly handed me the fish and removed the hook. Karen snapped several close-up pictures of the fish, the fish on the measuring tape, and pictures of me with the fish. The 26-inch little tunny was then swiftly dropped back into the ocean, and it swam away. Our team did a great job collecting the required information. The fish was later confirmed as the rod and reel Texas state catch and release record and also the fly rod catch and release state record resulting in two state records for a single fish.

Several states have a fly fishing record category that is separate from a traditional rod and reel record category. Other states include fly fishing in the rod and reel category or the pole and line record category. Rules and regulations regarding fly fishing change slightly between states. States often have a general statement that conventional fly fishing tackle and fly casting methods should be used. Some states prohibit the use of treble hooks or tandem hooks. The lure is usually defined as a recognized type of artificial fly. In general, the line should carry the fly, not the other way around. Scented flies or baiting the hook are prohibited when trying to achieve a fly fishing record.

For some species, the IGFA issues fly rod world records in tippet categories. Tippet class records are available for 2, 4, 6, 8, 12, 16, and 20 pound tippet. FFHF fly rod world records are also available for multiple tippet classes up to 50 pound tippet, and for unlimited tippet class for larger species. This creates the potential for an expansive number of world records. Both the IGFA and FFHF record requirements are specific, so check their websites for information. Tippet breaking strength is tested before a fly rod world record is issued.

UNCONVENTIONAL METHODS | 93

Fly fishing for freshwater species is becoming increasingly popular. Barry Osborn is holding his 34.25-inch fly fishing Texas catch and release state record, and FFHF catch and release world record common carp.

Fly fishing offers tremendous opportunities for setting records. Over the years, my background has allowed me to teach many anglers how to fly fish. Fly fishing is like many sports, and you can become an average fly fishing angler with little practice. With training, an inexperienced fly fishing angler has the ability to land a 25 plus inch fish on a fly rod within an hour of practice. Becoming an expert fly fishing angler is another story. It can take a lifetime to perfect the art of fly fishing, but each moment of learning is part of the fun.

Fly fishing record categories have been added to many state programs within the last decade, and there are still plenty of potential award categories that are vacant or have been filled with small fish that can easily be replaced. Fly fishing provides an excellent angling opportunity to achieve a fishing record, and multiple fish species can be effectively obtained utilizing this method. There are several books and websites available to help an angler learn how to fly fish.

5

AWARDS AND PROGRAMS

- ANNUAL AWARDS -

Our family vacation was coming to an end. We were visiting Yellowstone National Park in Wyoming. After completing the popular tours, everyone was tired. Wondering what we should do next, the other members of my family said they wanted to rest for a few hours. Karen looked at me and said, "This would be a good time to go fishing if you want to go." This year was one of those vacations where "we agreed" not to spend the majority of our vacation fishing…a "huge sacrifice" for me. A hook was not placed in the water the entire trip. Calmly answering my wife, I said, "Well I guess I could give it a try for a little while if everyone else wants to rest." The national park's speed limit may have been slightly exceeded while excitedly heading to Yellowstone Lake.

The black woolly bugger fly hit the water and disappeared out of sight. Stripping the line moved the fly steadily through the water. On the third cast, there was a pick-up, and the hook set initiated the fight. The fish swam one way and then the other, taking the line off the reel in short bursts. After maintaining constant pressure, the fish was brought to the net. A large grin appeared on my face as I admired the shimmering 19-inch cutthroat trout. After a few quick pictures, the fish was released. A nearby park ranger remarked that this was the largest cutthroat trout he had seen caught in the lake this season.

Unfamiliarity with cutthroat trout caused me to check the record books. The fish was considerably short of the state record. I remember thinking it would be nice to have an annual award system to recognize visiting anglers fishing in the park.

Many states have added annual award programs to recognize noteworthy catches made by anglers. These programs provide excellent opportunities to memorialize record fish. Usually, specific fish species are listed in an annual program, and there is a minimum size limit associated with each fish species.

Annual recognition programs are a great addition to a state's existing award program. Annual awards are reset each year allowing anglers yearly opportunities to receive records. Annual record programs exist for catch and release and waterbody records.

- JUNIOR ANGLERS -

The port line, rigged with an Atlantic cutlassfish, was trolling behind the boat. My 12-year-old daughter, Laura was piloting the boat and maintained a straight line headed toward a shrimp boat. My ten-year-old daughter, Cindy was sitting beside my wife Karen discussing unknown mother and daughter things. We were 25 miles off the coast with calm blue water in every direction.

The International Penn 12 reel began singing and the call "Fish on!" was heard from all quarters. It was Laura's turn, and she headed toward the rod. The drag on the reel was light, and climbing into the chair, Laura moved the drag forward slightly to a predetermined spot on the reel. The reel was still spinning as we clipped it to a cleat for safety purposes. Finally, the reel stopped screaming. Laura then began the process of lifting the rod up and down like a seasoned pro. Although it was one of her first times in the chair with a big fish, her practice paid off. After a lengthy fight, the fish and Laura were tiring. Although the leader was touched several times, each time the action was followed by a screaming reel. After a long battle, the worn out fish was grabbed by the tail, and the beautiful king mackerel was lifted into the boat. The fish was 56 inches long and weighed 38 pounds.

Not bad for my 55-inch tall daughter. After taking pictures and measurements, we released the fish and watched it swim away. We were ecstatic about Laura's ability to land the fish on her own.

Looking back at pictures of our family fishing trips is enjoyable. The king mackerel Laura caught would have remained as the junior angler saltwater state record for years. Due to my lack of knowledge concerning the record program, the paperwork was never submitted.

In states that separate adult and junior anglers, state junior angler record categories are typically wide open especially for other methods or unrestricted categories. Annual and waterbody records can easily be acquired by young anglers, and there are several lakes where a junior angler can set a record on almost every fishing trip. Similarly, there are IGFA world records readily available for junior anglers. By beginning at an early age, anglers have the ability to set hundreds of records over their lifetime of fishing.

Along with junior angler awards, many states have special awards for the first fish caught by an angler. Even if your state does not have state recognition, there are sites where you can get recognition for an angler that catches a memorable fish. The IGFA has both freshwater and saltwater certificates that are great for framing. Your children will appreciate looking back at these documents to remember their achievements. When my girls were young, it would have been nice to have submitted paperwork to memorialize their first fish.

Take a kid fishing. There is overwhelming satisfaction in watching and teaching a junior angler how to catch a fish. Children are the future of the sport, so invest your time in them.

- TOURNAMENTS -

The Destin Florida Fishing Rodeo was in full swing as Karen rested while we headed for our fishing location. The rodeo tournament runs the entire month of October and is open to all registered boats. We were fishing from a party boat that charges by the person. Red snapper, vermilion snapper, and greater amberjack are the usual fish taken on the trip. Karen had landed several nice red snapper and

98 | THE ART OF FISHING FOR RECORDS

Fishing records are readily available for junior anglers. Four-year-old Braxton Mosley is proudly holding his 12-pound common carp Lake Granbury junior angler record.

AWARDS AND PROGRAMS | 99

Catching one fish after another is fun and engaging for young anglers. Two-year-old Alexis Mosley is tickled while admiring her bluegill with "Papa" Barry Osborn.

vermilion snapper. After landing multiple red snapper, my fishing interest turned to greater amberjack. In addition to using my bottom rig, I often drift a flat line behind the boat. My gold Penn International 12 reel was spooled with 25-pound big game line rigged and ready for action. The reel contained a heavy steel leader with two Mustad 8/0 hooks. A 10-inch bait fish was placed on the rig and drifted behind the boat. The deckhand said, "You will never catch a fish on that rig. The 120-pound steel leader is too heavy and visible for the wary fish of Florida." He was correct for most of the day.

The trip was nearly over, and Karen was in the process of landing a greater amberjack when my Penn International 12 reel started screaming. Karen was fighting her fish and told me to grab the Penn rod. While disengaging the clicker, my concern grew as the line continued to burn off the reel. Karen caught her greater amberjack and was now standing next to me baiting her hook for another snapper.

The fish took over three-quarters of line off the reel before it finally stopped. The fish was extremely fast. My new problem was reeling fast enough to keep slack out of the line as the fish darted from one location to another. The eight-pound drag was well suited for the 25-pound big game line spooled on the reel, but it did not allow me to muscle the fish. I knew the fight was going to be a long back and forth battle. The deckhand came by after the hookup and told me he would be back when the fish was close to the boat.

The fish caused me to run back and forth across the stern of the boat several times involving maneuvers to go over and under the other anglers. The deckhand had observed much of the activity and came by again to see how I was enduring the fight. He looked at the half empty spool on the reel and asked me why it was taking so long to get in this bonita. I told him it did not feel like a bonita. He said, "We have very big bonita in this area." He left again to help another angler. When he returned, he found I had recovered most of the line on the reel. Still, he ribbed me further and said, "If you don't hurry up and get this fish in I am going to start calling you Sally." For the next ten minutes, he just said, "Sally" as he walked by. He threw in, "Maybe it's a blackfin tuna" on the next pass.

The fight was enjoyable, and eventually, I began gaining back line as the fish tired. The deckhand was still calling me "Sally" when the fish became visible behind the boat. He quickly changed his demeanor as he yelled out, "He's got a hoo! Everyone get your lines in!" The wahoo displayed a magnificent light show in the gentle rollers, flashing its colors while swimming back and forth behind the stern. There were hi-fives and cheers all around as the deckhand gaffed the wahoo and brought it onto the deck.

The 58-inch wahoo was not my biggest wahoo, and it would not place in the Destin rodeo wahoo division, but it was a nice fish. Although the wahoo did not place me in rodeo standings, if Karen had landed the wahoo she would have won the lady angler largest fish award caught on a party boat for that year.

Fishing tournaments are often associated with an image of an advertising billboard clad angler raising his arms while supporting two humongous largemouth bass. With over a hundred largemouth bass tournaments in the United States, these tournaments are a gratifying way to receive recognition. Countless books, magazines, and websites are devoted to largemouth bass fishing, including how anglers can achieve recognition during tournaments.

Largemouth bass tournaments are not the only fishing tournaments available to anglers. Fishing tournaments abound in the United States and throughout the world. There are tournament categories for specific waterbodies, fish species, largest fish, smallest fish, specific fishing methods, angler age, angler gender, and for just about any other fishing category that may spark your interest. Many tournaments, like the Coastal Conservation Association (CCA) Star Tournament, occur during specific times of the year. Almost every coastal state has some type of seasonal fishing rodeo or multi-day tournament.

Fishing tournaments are big business in the United States. With winnings accounting for millions of dollars in earnings, tournament popularity will continue. Tournaments are a terrific way to achieve angling recognition. You can select the level of involvement you wish to invest, but be advised that as award money increases the level of intensity usually increases. It may upset an angler if you cause the angler to lose a state record because you miss a fish with a gaff. It is more serious if your miss causes the loss of a million dollar prize or a boat. Although participation in fishing tournaments is exciting, these contests should be entered with care. Friendships can be either destroyed or gained while fishing in tournaments.

The overarching goal of most anglers in tournaments is to win money and recognition. Since documenting records is time-consuming, tournament anglers are usually not willing to lose precious time collecting data on fish that do not increase their chances of winning a tournament. Therefore, many potential state and world records are often lost during fishing tournaments.

One of my weird dreams is to fish in a big money largemouth bass tournament and catch a state record catfish or buffalo. It would be enjoyable to witness the reaction and expression on my fishing partner's face when my partner is asked to stop fishing to measure my fish and take a few photographs.

There are tournaments and promotions specifically devoted to catching records, and these can provide great opportunities to achieve fishing recognition. Many tournaments contain rules that allow anglers to record a world record fish caught in accordance with IGFA regulations. Tournaments often require a video of the catch so rule compliance can be confirmed. Always dedicate time to examine tournament rules before participating in these events. A simple or obscure rule can eliminate your winning catch.

- ORGANIZATIONS AND CONTESTS -

The boat moved slowly back and forth as the anchor line tightened on Wayne's 18-foot Kenner boat. My good friends, Wayne and Steve, were fishing in the back of the boat and my rods were in holders on the side rail. The few small southern flounder that found their way to my rods did not compare to the spotted seatrout that Steve and Wayne were constantly catching. The incoming tide brought blue water to the jetty, and striped mullet were actively swimming near the shoreline. Once again, Wayne's rod bent over hard as a big spotted seatrout nailed the mullet on the end of his line. After a good fight, we netted the 32-inch trophy spotted seatrout. Steve quickly followed Wayne's fish with a 30-inch spotted seatrout, and they each ended the day with five fish over 25 inches in length. Not a single spotted seatrout found its way to my hook the entire day, but I greatly improved my netting skills. Wayne caught the largest fish of the day and won the daily big fish award money contributed by all 12 anglers participating in the October annual fishing trip.

There are hundreds of angling organizations in the United States and throughout the world, ranging from highly organized clubs to a small group of friends who like to fish together. Many of these anglers have fished side-by-side for years. A group of fisherman from my office has fished together on the Texas coast every year for over 30 years. During these fishing excursions, our enthusiastic group has created competitions to add to the camaraderie of the trip, and it has been a fun learning experience to fish with this group over the years.

Fishing groups and organizations provide a great way to obtain recognition for anglers. There are freshwater organizations, saltwater organizations, and species-specific organizations throughout the world. Largemouth bass fishing organizations are the most well-known, but there are organizations that specialize in fishing for many different fish species found in North America. Organizations may adhere to specific techniques such as fly fishing, and other groups may only fish in certain waterbodies. The options are endless.

Several of these organizations have a sophisticated award and record program including record listings, pins, cash prizes, clothing, and certificates. Other organizations have less formal recognition, and achievements may only include bragging rights. Organizational awards and recognition can be an excellent supplement to the angling experience. Lifetime friendships are made when anglers with similar interests decide to spend their time fishing together.

Organizations and fishing groups often sponsor contests for specific species or for the largest fish. Manufacturers may provide contests for catching a fish using their line or tackle products. Sports television shows provide contests where they give away merchandise to the

Remember to participate in small recognition opportunities. This party boat lingcod caught in San Diego, California by Barry Osborn won the big fish prize money for the half-day trip.

winning angler. My fly rod catch and release state record red snapper photograph was submitted to the Fox Sports Outdoors Report television show. The sizeable fish enabled me to win the fish of the month award, and the prize was Costa Del Mar sunglasses. There are hundreds of contests providing awards and recognition.

Colleges and high schools are adding and expanding their fishing programs. Some high schools allow students to achieve a varsity letter for fishing. Fishing is included alongside football, golf, and other sports programs. College fishing organizations are one of the fastest-growing programs in the college curriculum, extending potential avenues for students to achieve fishing recognition and awards. Scholastic tournaments can provide anglers with accolades on a national level. Most of these programs concentrate on largemouth bass fishing. Because of the associated pleasure and monetary potential, many anglers have aspirations of turning their hobby into a profession. If you are willing to put in the work and learn the art of fishing, saltwater and freshwater opportunities exist for a career in this field.

Through intentional, premeditated planning, you may be the next angler to catch a record, win a new rod and reel, or even be awarded a new boat. Find an angling group or organization and become a member. There are organizations available at local, regional, national, and world levels. Investing time to learn about the sport can pay off with records, awards, and recognition.

- FITNESS PROGRAMS -

Dropping my backpack and resting for a few minutes felt good after the 10-mile hike to reach the Colorado mountain lake. The clear water of the lake reflected the snow-covered mountains in the distance. The slight breeze created a perfect condition for fishing. The backpack travel rod and reel felt good in my hand as I secured the reel on the rod. The bobber barely hit the water when it disappeared. After a quick hook set, a 16-inch rainbow trout was pulled onto the bank. It only took a few minutes to catch enough fish for dinner. Sitting near the fire, it was easy to hear the sound of trout fillets sizzling in the pan as the sun began to set behind the mountains. I smiled and thought to myself, "How does it get any better than this."

There are many benefits to exercising, and fishing is an excellent activity to develop physical fitness. In the age of computer games and smartphones, fishing is a wonderful source of exciting physical outdoor activity. Software programs, technological devices, and apps can be utilized to document any physical activity including fishing. Fishing programs are sponsored by various organizations including private, commercial, state, and national agencies and these organizations can help you reach your physical fitness and fishing goals.

The United States Department of Health and Human Services sponsors several fitness and nutrition programs associated with the President's Council on Fitness, Sports, and Nutrition. Depending on the program you participate in, you can receive recognition for a spectrum of physical activities including fishing. Under the Presidential Active Lifestyle Award (PALA+), fishing activities can be recorded with the PALA+ paper log to provide recognition for anglers. The website information for PALA+ is located at hhs.gov.

Anyone six years and older can participate in the PALA+ program. The program is based on activity and nutrition. Recognition is based on nutritional goals and the amount of time an activity is conducted per week. Once you successfully complete the six to eight-week program, you can receive recognition. Currently, you can order certificates, shirts, and other products to reflect your accomplishments. PALA+ provides an excellent opportunity for young and old anglers to engage in a physical and nutritional goal-oriented program. Fishing is one of the many activities PALA+ accepts.

Fitness programs are often changed, modified, absorbed into existing programs, or become discontinued. One of my favorite fitness programs was the President's Challenge program. After documenting my fishing activities for 11 years, I received a Presidential Champions Platinum Award Medal and a signed certificate from the President of the United States recognizing my accomplishments. Unfortunately, like many government programs, the President's Challenge program was ultimately discontinued.

AWARDS AND PROGRAMS | 107

Participating in private or government fitness programs is a way to receive recognition for fishing. Barry Osborn received these awards through the President's Challenge Program for his fishing activities spanning 11 years.

Search the internet to discover physical fitness programs, and determine if fishing qualifies as an accepted activity. Although these programs come and go, they can provide recognition opportunities.

- MULTI-SPECIES AWARDS -

We were anchored a few miles off the coast, and Karen had already caught her limit of red snapper for the day. Only one more snapper was needed to complete my limit when three large green, yellow, and blue fish swam up behind the boat. Quickly throwing chum to the fish kept them in the area as they rapidly gobbled it up. A Garcia 7000 reel was ready and waiting in a rod holder for such an occasion. My squid sailed past the trio, and a bull dolphin whirled engulfing the bait. The hook set was successful, and the aerial show began. The bull dolphin repeatedly jumped and dove deep until the exhausted fish was coaxed back toward the boat. Two cow dolphins were swimming beside the male, so the hooked bull dolphin was left in the water allowing the other anglers to have a chance to catch one.

Everyone else was fishing with a heavy steel leader, and the cows would not take their offerings. Suddenly my dolphin came to life and shot under the boat jumping right behind the engine. The line hit the propeller, and the fish broke off. Not to be deterred, a bare hook was quickly tied on the line embellished by a piece of cut bait and thrown to the remaining dolphin. One of the cows immediately grabbed the baited hook. When I got the female dolphin to the boat, she was alone. The 33-inch fish was hooked through the gills and bleeding, so we harvested her and did not turn her in for a state catch and release award. The dolphin still qualified as a big fish award counting as one of the five big fish I needed toward my saltwater elite angler award.

Multi-species awards are increasing in popularity. Grand slam awards have been around for decades, and the combination of species qualifying for grand slam awards has expanded. Local slam records vary greatly and are often defined according to the area where fishing occurs. Fishing in the middle coastal area of Texas may result in a slam consisting of red drum, spotted seatrout, and southern flounder.

AWARDS AND PROGRAMS | 109

Karen Osborn achieved ten big fish awards and was the first woman to receive both a Texas saltwater and freshwater elite angler award.

Fishing further south along the coast, common snook may replace southern flounder in the slam. Freshwater slams for trout will also vary depending on the species available in a specific area and the organization overseeing the grand slam record. Typically grand slams consist of three or four fish species landed within a specific period of time from a day, to a season, to a lifetime. Many anglers view grand slam awards as the ultimate recognition. The IGFA has formalized their slam record categories and recognizes ten grand slam three species awards, and ten super grand slam four species awards, for fish taken in a single day. They also have six royal slam clubs for certain species achieved over the course of one's lifetime.

Several states have created programs to recognize anglers that obtain multi-species awards for catching record size fish consisting of different species. Most of these programs allow an angler a lifetime to achieve these awards, but some programs are established for annual fishing records. Names like master angler, elite angler, and trophy angler are used to identify anglers that attain these awards. Multi-species awards are difficult to earn because an angler usually concentrates on a specific area or species. Completing a multi-species award requires an angler to be proficient in a variety of fishing techniques in different locations. Multi-species awards are often the most difficult angling awards to achieve under a state fishing program.

6

SECRETS TO SUCCESS

- VACANT OR OPEN CATEGORIES -

The high definition television displayed the vivid blue colors of a yellowfin tuna as the deckhand reached for the gaff. My morning was spent watching people catching fish instead of fishing. A question began to materialize in my mind. Given enough time and with a little research, can an angler catch record fish on a consistent basis? As the show ended, my computer hummed as my research began. One concept that became readily apparent was that the quickest way to achieve a record is to find an open or vacant fish record category. My quest to regularly target fishing records and to expand my knowledge about the art of fishing for records ensued.

For the majority of the anglers on the party boat, this was a normal trip. Personally, I planned to end the day with a state record catch. The main target species of the charter trip was vermilion snapper since red snapper season was closed. My wife Karen stood next to me and was lifting two vermilion snapper over the gunnel when a sharksucker swam out from under the boat to grab a piece of chum. Sharksuckers commonly swim under boats when offshore fishing, so this was not an unusual sighting. A handline with a hook attached was already rigged and waiting in my tackle bag. A squid head was secured on the Mustad UltraPoint hook and the hook, line, and squid cleared the gunnel on the way to the water.

Our friend Captain Tim looked at me and said, "Ok, what record are you after this time." Captain Tim is a world record and state record holder, and we have discussed catching records on many occasions. He knew if my hook went in the water in some unusual way a record was a possibility. I smiled as the sharksucker raced toward my bait and grabbed my squid. After a quick line wrap and tug, the fish was on. The fight was short, and the hand over hand action brought the fish into the boat. The sharksucker record was vacant, so the medium sized 2.9-pound, 26.25-inch fish qualified as the new state record in the unrestricted category with a handline.

After a successful fishing trip, a list was generated of both freshwater and saltwater fish species and several record possibilities became apparent. There were vacant spots available for various species on the state fish and wildlife department lists throughout the United States. The IGFA world record database provided a list indicating vacant categories for both freshwater and saltwater species. The FFHF official world freshwater angling record publication included open categories for several species that did not have a posted record.

In the process of locating vacant records, to my astonishment, there was a public lake near my home that did not have any fish records documented. This lake was constructed six years earlier, and it had just opened up for fishing. Therefore, every fish caught over a half of a pound would qualify as a lake waterbody record.

The sun was rising, and excitement was building as we headed for the lake. Karen loves to fish with earthworms, and she held the small cooler containing the worms on her lap. We arrived at the lake and rigged up our poles to fish from the shore. My rods were still lying on a picnic table as the water rippled when Karen's bobber disappeared under the surface. A scale and a measuring board were ready and waiting as she pulled in a large lake record bluegill. A few minutes later, Karen's largemouth bass erupted from the water shaking its head as it tried to dislodge the Mustad hook. The fish was landed quickly and was soon followed by four more largemouth bass between the two of us. The activity of catching bluegill and largemouth bass was regularly interrupted as we landed several channel catfish.

Fishing was outstanding all day, and we landed ten potential records for three species of fish. We both were able to replace the record fish we had landed earlier in the day with larger fish. The highlight of the trip was when Karen caught a channel catfish weighing close to my existing potential record channel catfish. After she placed her fish on the scale, she looked at me and said, "Oh, my fish is bigger." Then she smiled and gave me a quick kiss.

We fished the lake again a couple of days later, and although we could have turned in several records from the first day of fishing, we decided to only record the three largest fish caught including a 3.7-pound channel catfish, a 3.7-pound largemouth bass, and a 0.6-pound bluegill. Since the lake had recently opened for fishing, it was not listed on the Texas Parks and Wildlife Department record site. We sent a letter to the parks and wildlife department requesting that they add the lake to the waterbody record list and include our records. They complied, and once the lake and our records were listed, other anglers began submitting records for the lake including rod and reel, fly fishing, and catch and release records. Because of the small size of our fish, all of our records were replaced except for Karen's bluegill that has remained the waterbody record since 2011.

Not all states or agencies maintain waterbody records, but for those that do it amazes me how many lakes, rivers, ponds, and bays do not contain documented record fish. Finding a vacant record for a specific species on a current record list, or an open record on a waterbody is an excellent way to target record fish resulting in certificates for an angler. To determine if there is a vacant record category for a specific waterbody or fish species, research the historical records for the area where you will be fishing. Look at each record category and determine if there is a species missing for a particular line weight, method, or location. If there are waterbody records available for the area, and the lake is not listed, then you may have a golden opportunity to achieve a record catch.

Consider taking the time to visit with local game wardens and biologists. They are often aware of fish species regularly caught but not documented in an existing record list. Different fishing methods

Understanding record categories increase your chances for a record. Barry Osborn's almaco jack state record on a fly rod filled a vacant category on the Texas record list.

such as bowfishing or fly fishing may result in vacant categories and available records. Special attention should be given to junior anglers since many states have separate lists devoted to them. Historically, the IGFA has separated men and women saltwater record categories, so vacant categories may exist for one gender but not for the other. Recently they separated the genders for freshwater species opening hundreds of potential world record opportunities for women.

- RESEARCH AND PLANNING -

Winter was approaching, and my research of the surrounding lakes indicated that Lake Lewisville in Texas was the most desirable lake in the area to find a trophy blue catfish, so we booked a guided trip. Karen still needed four fish to complete her Texas freshwater elite angler award, but only one big fish award was needed to complete my multi-species freshwater elite angler award. Landing a freshwater big fish record would make me the second person in the state of Texas to be recognized with both a saltwater and freshwater elite angler award. Although we had a fantastic trip that day, including adding several fish to the ice chest, neither of us caught a fish large enough to count toward our freshwater elite angler award.

Through a careful review of the Texas Parks and Wildlife Department big fish award list, and by taking into account the time of year and the size of fish needed for each species, we determined blue catfish to be the best species to pursue during the winter months. Catching a 36-inch blue catfish appeared to be the best way to achieve a big fish award. Lake Tawakoni was only a few miles from Lake Lewisville and was known for having more trophy-sized blue catfish. However, our guide at Lake Lewisville had worked diligently to find us trophy fish on our previous trip. He knew we were after a record and he was aware of the restrictions required to catch one. We gave him a call and booked another trip to Lake Lewisville.

Typical of January weather, there was a cold front forecast. The next day was going to be a warm winter day, and the guide had a cancellation, so I took leave from work to fish before the weather changed. The forecast indicated the wind at the beginning of the day would be low but would increase throughout the day before the front. Usually, these conditions result in a good day of fishing or a severe lack of bites. Karen was looking forward to another chance at a big fish, and all of us including our guide were feeling anticipation and excitement for another opportunity for a record. After anchoring, the guide cut shad for bait and soaked each piece with attractant spray. Early morning fishing was slow, but by mid-morning both of us had landed several nice blue catfish weighing up to ten pounds. A 36-inch blue catfish still eluded us, but we all felt we would have at least one chance at a fish of this size before the charter trip was over.

The golden opportunity came on my end of the boat. The guide yelled "Fish!" as the back rod bent over hard with the tip almost touching the water. The line was screaming off the reel and moving toward the propeller. Hurriedly, my hand reached for the rod. Unfortunately, my feet did not cooperate, and I slipped as I struggled to get the rod out of the holder. The rod came free, and I instinctively jerked it to set the hook and move the line away from the propeller. After a few more cranks on the reel, it was apparent there was no longer any resistance. The fish was gone. Turning toward the guide, although he was trying to cover it up, you could see the disappointment on his face.

We were using circle hooks, and although we will never know for sure why the fish came unhooked, my jerk probably pulled the circle hook free from the fish's mouth. It was a rookie mistake. The guide indicated we would get the next one, but having been a guide myself, I knew he was a little frustrated. He had been up very early preparing for the day by catching threadfin shad and gizzard shad for bait. He knew we were after a record, and he did his best to plan out our day accordingly. My actions let us all down. He was gracious and uplifting with his comments, but we both knew I probably just lost the fish that would have completed my freshwater elite angler award.

Fortunately, the day was only half over. With building winds, we headed for a new location. After rebaiting our rods with shad, we were fishing once again. A lull in the action gave us time to eat a quick sandwich, and we were refreshed and ready to "rock and roll."

While observing a fisherman on the bank, a twitch in my rod tip caught my eye. Moving toward the rod, the line went slack and then quickly tightened. Turning the handle on the reel as the rod cleared the holder, the pull on the end of the line was strong…fish on!

As my rod bent over, the pull was met with an opposing force in the opposite direction. The reel squealed loudly as it gave up line. I methodically used a pumping action to regain some line back on the reel. The fish was moving toward the boat. The guide had a net in hand as he watched the battle waiting in anticipation.

The fight wore on, and the fish was nearly to the boat when the rod beside me bent over hard. Starting to reach for that rod to tighten the line the guide yelled, "No, stay on your fish!" My concentration turned back to the fish on my line as the rod next to me showed no further signs of a bite. As my fish rolled on the surface, the guide's concern over the fish became apparent. It was a big fish.

After the blue catfish rolled, it dove down below the boat, and a head-shake indicated displeasure as it tried to dislodge the hook. Tension on the line was maintained as the fish came up again rolling next to the boat. Everyone was relieved when the guide netted the fish and lifted it out of the water. There were quick high-fives all around even before the fish hit the deck. Our excitement was confirmed as we slid the big blue catfish on a measuring board. The fish measured 37.25 inches and weighed 26.4 pounds. I was now a pending freshwater elite angler record holder.

The record blue catfish was the result of ample research and planning that had occurred before we booked our trip and continued until the day we fished. We specifically communicated with our guide concerning our goal to catch a trophy blue catfish over 36 inches in length. He was honest and direct and told us the best time to catch a trophy blue catfish was in the winter. Based on this information, we delayed our trip by six months until January. Although fishing in the summer may have resulted in a larger quantity of smaller fish, deciding to postpone our trip until the winter months increased the probability of us catching a blue catfish that would be longer than the length needed to obtain my award.

If your goal is to achieve fishing records, adequate planning and research is essential. Barry Osborn's 2.3-pound gray triggerfish resulted in a Texas fly fishing state record.

Any fishing endeavor can yield a record catch. Record fish can be caught in the most unlikely situations. Checking the record books to select a fishing location that has previously contained trophy fish will increase your chances of landing a record. To determine a desirable fishing area, you should consider documented records, stocking records, the age of the lake, fishing reports, and have conversations with other anglers who fish the location regularly. Waterbodies are constantly changing, so a productive lake from the past may not be a suitable location to catch a record at the present time.

The time of year, record availability, fishing location, type of bait, regulations, and the fishing method should all be considered when chasing a record. Although planning may lead you to concentrate on a specific species, do not eliminate other species as viable options. Many record fish are caught unexpectedly while an angler is concentrating on an entirely different species. For example, while fishing coastal bay waters, it is a good idea to have an extra rod with live bait or cut bait drifting behind the boat while other anglers are casting artificial lures. Utilizing knowledge concerning various species and diversifying your methods will result in landing more record fish.

Throughout the United States, largemouth bass are one of the most sought-after species. For this reason, it is challenging to catch a largemouth bass record in most states while using a rod and reel. This fact should not keep you from pursuing a record largemouth bass if that is your goal. On the other hand, do not expect to catch a largemouth bass record quickly by utilizing a rod and reel. Learning the art of fishing with other methods opens opportunities for achieving a largemouth bass record. A state record largemouth bass was one of the fish on my bucket list, so I decided to change my approach. This change allowed me to catch several state record largemouth bass using the Plnor fishing method.

Some documented record fish are so massive that even with research, planning, and a considerable amount of luck, a lifetime of fishing may be required to replace an existing record. Therefore unless you are devoted to a particular species, pursuing fish within normal weight and length ranges will increase the odds of accomplishing

120 | THE ART OF FISHING FOR RECORDS

Planning improves your ability to catch a variety of species. Ken and Kim Laterza are featured with a blacktip shark, a cobia, Spanish mackerel, little tunny, and red snapper. One of Kim's red snappers resulted in a big fish award.

your record goals. This logic is useful in relation to all record levels including waterbody records, state records, and world records in all categories. By taking this stance to the extreme, you will find it is easy to replace existing records of some species because the documented fish are well below the normal weight or length. If you want a quick record, then concentrate on those species.

- RULE CHANGES -

The flooded lake water appeared chocolate brown and contained large amounts of floating logs and debris. You could hear the slurping noise as common carp were actively sampling potential food items on the water's surface. Assembling my fly rod, the pieces slid together easily. The goal of the day was to catch a big fish toward my freshwater elite angler award. Recent lobbying from local anglers resulted in the Texas Parks and Wildlife Department adding common carp to the big fish award catch and release species list. There was a vacant category for this record, and this location has produced hundreds of common carp over the years. A record for a common carp over 30 inches was within reach. The day was primed for an opportunity to gain a big fish award and a catch and release record at the same time.

Upon reaching the shore, it was obvious conditions were perfect. Schools of five to ten common carp could be seen rolling in varying locations along the surface. The second cast of my elk hair fly tied on a Mustad hook produced a clean hookup. After reeling in the catch, the fish was 28 inches in length, just two inches shy of my goal. The fish swam away hastily after being released. The morning action was fast and furious and ended with 27 fish netted, including the 30-inch common carp needed for my big fish award. This fish qualified toward my multi-species freshwater elite angler award certification and was the catch and release lake record.

Continually monitor your state's fish and wildlife department rules concerning fishing awards and records. Significant changes have transpired in states' angling programs in recent years. Some of these changes have made it more difficult to set records while other changes

Multiple species of fish will consume a fly, and often anglers do not realize these species are available to obtain a fly fishing record. Barry Osborn is holding a Texas fly fishing catch and release state record, 25.25-inch red snapper.

have made it easier. If you do not know the rules, you may be losing out on potential records including potential world records. Some rules contain complicated and seemingly contradictory language, and you can use this to your advantage. By assimilating information about different species and regulations, you may be able to document a record on a species that has not been recorded.

With the recreational value of fishing in the billions, many states have expanded their recognition programs. Catch and release categories, fly fishing categories, and annual award programs have been added to stimulate interest in fishing. If you are not satisfied with the fishing program in your state, contact the fish and wildlife department and ask them to expand the angler recognition program. Employees of these departments are often accommodating, hard-working individuals and avid anglers. Search until you find a champion of the program who is willing to help. Although all state programs are political animals, public interest may be all that is needed to broaden and expand a state's award and record recognition program.

- FIRST AND LAST LIGHT -

The cool morning air caused me to hunker down behind the boat's windshield as we headed up the lake. It was still dark, but there was a faint orange color beginning to form on the horizon. The sky was filled with spectacular colors over one of my favorite fishing spots. It was early spring, and the white bass and striped bass were chasing threadfin shad onto a rocky point while violently feeding on them near the surface of the water. The past couple of weeks were productive, and similar results were expected this morning.

The anchor settled to the bottom, and the boat swung around within easy casting distance of the shore. The old 6/7 weight Browning fly rod felt comfortable in my hand as the line was stripped onto the deck. The deceiver fly barely hit the water when the first wave of white bass busted the surface. The next cast caused the chartreuse and white fly to land on the edge of the froth. Immediately a nice 15-inch white bass engulfed it. My freezer was already full of fish, so the plan was to release my fish. Although this fish would have been a new lake record on a fly, I did not have a scale available, and I did not want to kill the fish for a waterbody record. After being released, the white bass swam away quickly when it was dropped back into the water.

The next 45 minutes of fishing resulted in non-stop action. Over 25 white bass and one striped bass were brought to the net on a fly. As quickly as it started the action was over, and the water became calm again. Just like the past few days, the bite was over, and the sun was barely above the horizon. The next 30 minutes did not yield a single bite. This area is a popular fishing location, and soon other boats began arriving. It was a beautiful morning, and some of my fishing gear needed work, so I decided to work on my rods in the boat instead of heading for the dock.

My dog sat beside me while I pulled out my tackle box and worked on my fishing rods. We occasionally glanced at the other boats to see if they had any results. Not a single fish was caught, and after a couple of hours, the situation remained unchanged. The next morning would result in the same spectacular fishing action at first light, but for now, the fishing was over.

Once my tackle was organized, we headed home to do some tasks around the house. After completing most of my honey-do list, the potential of an evening feeding frenzy drew me back to my morning spot. It was about an hour and a half before dark, and the anchor settled just a few feet from where the morning action had occurred. Most of the boats from the morning were gone, but one boat was within talking distance. The anglers indicated they had been in the area all day and had only caught one fish. In addition, they had only witnessed two fish being caught by all the other boats.

I informed the anglers about the prime feeding frenzy times, which occur early and late each day, but they were tired and wanted to get their boat out of the water before dark. As these anglers left, the remaining two boats followed. The first wave of white bass came by about 45 minutes before dark. My fly landed a few feet from the shore as a white bass busted the shad along the shoreline, and immediately a fish hooked up…

Fishing early in the morning and late in the evening improves your opportunities to catch record fish. As a bonus, you will experience some gorgeous sunrises and sunsets.

Both freshwater and saltwater species of fish can be landed during all times of the day, but the most exhilarating fishing trips usually include the hours just before sunrise or sunset. Many anglers miss the best time of day to catch fish and the more fish you catch, the greater your chances are of catching a record.

Fish feeding times are based on genetics and conditions. If a fish actively bites during the same timeframe when most anglers are fishing, then it is more likely to be caught and removed from the population. However, a fish that feeds when anglers are not around is more likely to survive. For me, this scenario has proven to be true in several instances while fishing offshore. Typically for safety reasons and convenience, many offshore anglers prefer to return to port before it gets dark. Boats usually begin leaving fishing grounds and oil rigs three to four hours before the sun goes down. If an angler is willing to wait until most of the other boats have given up and decides to fish at dusk, the fish will usually begin biting. Many coolers have been filled with limits of big red snapper when anglers apply this method. Although this strategy does not always end in success, it does increase your chances of catching a record fish.

If you fish at first light, or into the evening, make sure your equipment is in good condition. Keep a watchful eye on the weather. Safety is more important than achieving any record catch, so plan ahead and be prepared for varying circumstances.

- BAIT, LURE, LOCATION -

The warm summer weather and the holiday weekend resulted in a crowded lake. Fish became active at first light with white bass frantically feeding along a rocky point. My limit of white bass was placed in the cooler. With a large fish fry planned, my focus switched to striped bass to ensure ample fish filets and provide variety. While heading to the lake's hot water outlet, boats were scattered throughout the lake. Warm water flowed from an electric plant through a channel allowing it to enter the lake via a small cove. A cable fence prevented boats from getting close to the churning water as it rolled over a weir.

When the electric plant was generating, the hot water outlet was a popular fishing location. The outlet fence was lined with boats including bass boats, Jon boats, and deck boats. The boats tied to the fence were nearly touching as anglers cast lines in all directions. Fortunately, a boat pulled away from the fence allowing a small space for my boat to slip in. The angler next to me said "hello" and indicated that fishing had been slow all day. A lady on the other side of my boat chimed in and said, "It has been really, really slow." Her fellow angler then said, "We've been here all morning, and we have only seen one small largemouth bass and one sand bass caught."

This was a regular fishing spot for me, and their report did not adversely affect my anticipation. Throwing a cast net, the net spread open across the water then sank. It returned with six medium sized gizzard shad. The shad were quickly placed inside the live well, and I rigged one rod with a two-ounce egg weight, a 5/0 Mustad hook, and a shad. I hooked the bait through the hard part of the nose to ensure it would stay on the line while swimming in the water. I cast my hook with the live shad toward the weir and placed my rod in a rod holder on the fence post that supported the cable.

Grabbing another rod with a large three-ounce silver slab spoon, the spoon was launched with maximum strength to span the 55 yards and reach the churning water. The spoon landed on the side of the weir and was carried into the white water below. Quickly reeling in the slack line resulted in a tug and a striped bass was hooked. The fish fought well in the moving water and took several minutes to land. The striped bass weighed ten pounds and was placed alongside my white bass in the ice chest.

After another long cast, a smaller striped bass immediately hooked up. Although this fish was not as large as the first one, it was still a decent size. Adding the fish to the cooler, it appeared there might be enough fish for the upcoming fish fry. The decision became moot as the screaming reel on the rod in the holder interrupted my thought process. Reaching for the rod, the lady next to me said, "You've got to be kidding." The Mustad hook did the job, and the rod bent over hard. This was a strong fighting fish. The biggest problem was trying to avoid the lines of other anglers as they attempted to cast into the frothing water below the weir. The nice 18-pound striped bass finally reached the net, and I had plenty of food for the fish fry.

While picking up my gear and preparing to leave, it became apparent that none of the other anglers had equipment that could reach the weir. I offered my slab spoon to the other anglers. Surprisingly, there were no takers. After untying from the fence, an angler said, "Unbelievable." as I pulled away.

This story is an extreme example of a successful fishing trip. There have been many occasions when an angler beside me caught fish after fish while my lure was never touched. The purpose of this story is to indicate how important it is to fish where the fish are biting and to utilize a method that will result in a productive catch. Typically after fishing for an hour without a bite, you should change your technique or move on. To this day, it is difficult for me to follow this rule since fishing with a large amount of equipment makes the process of moving inconvenient and time-consuming. A significant condition change, such as a tide change, is an exception to this rule if the change results in fish moving into the area where you are fishing.

Spend time researching the species you are after. Pay attention to the time of year, weather, food availability, time of day, cover, and water elevation. Visit with local anglers at bait and tackle stores to see what methods are working in the area. Do not be afraid to change equipment and techniques if a method is not productive. Be flexible. If you intend to fish for striped bass while white bass are chasing shad to the surface, consider fishing for white bass. A white bass record is just as good as a striped bass record. Catching fish may be more important than setting records, especially when fishing with other anglers. As a general rule, do not leave biting fish to go after other fish since this can jeopardize your success for the rest of the day. You are more likely to set a record while catching fish.

Another basic rule is that large bait results in large fish. We all have stories of huge fish caught on small bait or lures. However, the large bait rule does apply, especially when saltwater fishing. Using this logic you may use bait that is too large for a specific species, but when

SECRETS TO SUCCESS | 129

Utilizing natural bait is a great way to catch records. Learn to use a cast net to boost record prospects in both saltwater and freshwater.

striving after fishing records, it is best to use the largest bait a fish can swallow versus small bait or lures. A captain in Hawaii told me one reason more anglers do not catch grander (1000 pound plus) blue marlin is because they do not use 50-pound yellowfin tuna as bait. You will not catch as many fish if you use huge bait, but the fish will typically be larger with greater potential to achieve a record.

Research what a specific species of fish is eating in a particular area and take into account the time of year. Try to understand daily feeding pattern changes and weather conditions. Depending on conditions, fish may like eating dead shad at certain times of the year, while at other times they desire live shad. There are days when a red drum will not touch a topwater lure but will nail a gold spoon. The time of day or weather changes can cause the opposite to be true.

While fishing with a friend and tournament largemouth bass angler, it was astonishing to see the number of times he changed lures as he searched for the one with the right color patterns and action to entice a fish to bite. Once he started catching fish, he stuck with that method until the fish stopped biting, indicating it was time to change lures. It took several hours for him to identify what fish were feeding on, but once he determined the correct technique, it was fairly easy to get fish to strike his lure.

Always pay close attention to what is working. If you see someone catch a fish, then watch what that angler is doing. It is useful to ask for advice from other anglers who are creating results. If an angler catches three fish in a row and you have not caught a fish, then it may be time to change your methods. On any given day fish can have a small or large search image they use to trigger feeding. If their search pattern is broad, you can catch fish on almost anything, but if it is narrow then lure type, bait color, size, and shape will make a huge difference when catching fish and setting records.

In some cases, there may be little information available on how to catch a specific species, and conflicting information may be common. Blue tilapia were inadvertently introduced to a lake in my area, so I began the process of seeking out the best way to catch these fish with a hook and line. One article suggested tilapia could not be caught with

Search for birds feeding on the water's surface since this may indicate predatory fish below.

a hook and line, while another article indicated a hook and line was effective with a small piece of earthworm as bait. Still another article indicated a cast net was the only solution for harvesting these fish.

Many days of fishing with different baits were needed before finding a type of bait effective for catching big tilapia in this particular reservoir. Earthworms were occasionally effective for small fish but rarely resulted in landing a large specimen. Tilapia are usually considered to be vegetarians, so broccoli, corn, trout nuggets, and several other baits were all tried with little success. Finally, I tried a thumbnail-sized piece of freshwater drum cut-bait on a small, strong hook. The rig was a simple egg sinker held with a slip shot six to twelve inches above the hook. By utilizing cut-bait, and different fishing methods, several blue tilapia were landed including multiple state records. Trial and error is sometimes the best method for catching record fish.

- URBAN FISHING -

The surrounding skyscrapers and noisy automobiles contrasted the soothing sound of the water flowing down the river. The river bank was lined with anglers fishing downstream from the interstate bridge. Karen stood beside me on a platform fishing over the rock wall in front of us. The target species was rainbow trout, stocked in the river two days before. We fished for hours and watched as other anglers pulled in several rainbow trout, but neither of us caught a fish. Finally, we started to land an occasional 12-inch fish, much smaller than the 15-inch fish Karen needed for her big fish award.

It was nearly dark when Karen received a bite. She worked the fish toward the wall, and a rainbow trout was pulled into the net. The length of the fish was 15.25 inches and qualified for a big fish award and applied toward Karen's multi-species freshwater elite angler award. We attempted to release the fish but realized the rainbow trout was not going to survive. The catch and release award was eliminated, so we added another fish to the cooler. The river's waterbody record was vacant, so we weighed the fish, and at only 1.33 pounds the fish was recorded as a waterbody record for the river.

SECRETS TO SUCCESS | 133

Urban fishing areas are often ignored and can contain large fish. Barry Osborn's 4.75-pound, 22.5-inch state record rainbow trout was caught on the Trinity River in downtown Fort Worth, Texas using the Plnor method.

Many species of fish are stocked throughout the United States. Several states stock fish to increase fishing opportunities for urban anglers. Trout are stocked for year around fishing or as put-and-take species in areas of the country where they do not survive in the summer. Walleye, bluegill, striped bass, largemouth bass, and several other species of freshwater fish are stocked. Saltwater species such as red drum and spotted seatrout are stocked in coastal states. Stocking fish usually increases the chances for fishing records.

Although some states prohibit records for hatchery and stocked fish, other states allow stocked fish to qualify as records. In states where stocked fish can be documented as records, they are often overlooked. If you are seeking a world record, the IGFA indicates that applications will not be accepted for fish caught in hatchery waters, sanctuaries, or bodies of water stocked with fish for commercial purposes. The FFHF prohibits records from fish caught in hatchery waters and private waterbodies not accessible to the general public.

In conjunction with stocked areas, there are literally thousands of waterbodies available for fishing in urban areas. Many of these waterbodies are infrequently fished and contain record fish. Universities, parks, businesses, and housing subdivisions may maintain waterbodies that support big fish so do not overlook small waterbodies. These sites may be open to the public for fishing and often accommodate much larger fish than expected. These sites may also contain a species of fish not readily available in other waterbodies. Make sure to gain legal access to the areas where you fish.

- GUIDES -

The alarm went off at 3:30 a.m., and we rolled out of bed. For my wife getting up that early is always a struggle since she loves her morning rest. Thankfully the morning was warm, and the weather was good. It looked like it was going to be a great day for fishing. Karen was excited to get to the lake to meet our guide. We booked a trip to catch striped bass and hybrid striped bass. Hybrid striped bass are a cross between a striped bass and a white bass. They are often called hybrid bass or hybrids but are identified as whiterock bass by the IGFA and FFHF. Our goal was to catch fish that qualified for a big fish award adding to our multi-species freshwater elite angler award qualifications. We were fishing on Lake Tawakoni in north central Texas which has a reputation for producing large hybrid striped bass. To qualify for a big fish award, a hybrid striped bass must be at least 25 inches in total length.

Although the forecast was for a mild day, it turned out to be a hot July day. Our guide knew we were pursuing records. He met us at the dock before light, and we started fishing in a popular spot over submerged humps. We counted 37 boats in the area. Although the action normally starts at first light, today was an exception, and the fishing was slow. We fished diligently, but the striped bass and hybrid striped bass were not feeding. Finally, the guide suggested we fish in shallow water for white bass. Being a firm believer in fishing for what is biting, and since white bass were hitting the surface, we headed toward the shore. Reaching into my bag, I removed the big fish award qualification list. A 15-inch white bass was needed for a big fish award. Because there was a vacant white bass category, there was a good chance at setting a catch and release waterbody record, a big fish award, and a waterbody record for white bass. Although we planned to catch a record hybrid striped bass, it appeared we both had an excellent chance of catching a record white bass.

As we approached 12 feet of water, the guide turned the boat toward fish splashing on the surface. Karen was the first angler with a line in the water, and before completing my first cast, she called out "Fish on!" The bend in the rod indicated she had a big fish. The camera, scale, and measuring board were ready as she pulled the fish on board. The white bass was 15.75 inches in length and qualified as the second fish in her freshwater elite angler award qualification. The fish also qualified for the catch and release lake record. Pictures were taken of the fish lying on the measuring board and of Karen holding her fish. The white bass was released and swam away into the depths below. We had one pending record and plenty of time left during the day to fill our boat with fish.

Karen landed several more fish before my first pending record fish hit the deck. The fight was short and unimpressive. The white bass measured 16.50 inches in total length. My wife was excited for me even after she realized my fish replaced her earlier pending waterbody catch and release record. The catch also added a fish to my freshwater elite angler qualification. Neither of us landed a qualifying hybrid striped bass. However, by shifting our methods, relying on our guide, and pursuing feeding fish, we were both able to catch a record.

Utilizing guides is an efficient way to find record fish for a specific species. Successful guides are familiar with the landscape, fish movements, biting patterns, and the best types of bait. The cost of a guide service and fishing in close quarters on a boat are the biggest drawbacks when fishing with a guide. Most guides try to make the fishing day a pleasant experience, and many anglers utilize guides to avoid the costs and time associated with purchasing and maintaining their own boat. If you only fish a few times a year, fishing with a guide can be an effective way to obtain records.

Compared to fishing on your own, there is a loss of flexibility when fishing with a guide. Various types of guided trips are available ranging from party boats that can carry over 100 anglers to personal charter boats that accommodate two to six anglers. Party boats are less expensive, but there are more anglers to contend with, and tangled lines can result in losing record fish. On party boats, there is less help from the captain and deckhands since their time is split between multiple anglers. Overcrowding can make it difficult to collect the data and other information needed to document a record. Even under these conditions, several of my records were acquired while fishing from a party boat including a large 22.8-pound red drum with the pole and line no reel (Plnor) method. In addition, my wife has set several records from a party boat including a 27.75-inch red snapper Texas state catch and release record.

Private charters are wonderful, but they are usually more expensive, especially in saltwater. These boats frequently accommodate two to six anglers, and there may be opportunities to split the cost with another group. Personal charters give you the ability to tailor your

In certain circumstances, fishing with charter party boats yields record opportunities, and methods other than a rod and reel may be permitted. An eight hour trip out of Dolphin Docks in Port Aransas, Texas resulted in three state records for Barry Osborn including a 30.4-pound king mackerel on a fly rod, a 3.0-pound vermilion snapper on a fly rod, and a 2.9-pound sharksucker using a handline.

trip to find a record and provide outstanding opportunities to catch fish while learning new fishing techniques. If you make it a goal to acquire a new fishing method, technique, or skill from every charter trip, you will become proficient in the art of fishing for records.

Do research to find a qualified guide. Consider multiple sources of information to make your decision. Check available records and potential fishing locations to determine the species of record fish you seek. It is best to choose a guide that concentrates on a specific species of fish. Look at the guide's webpage and pay attention to the picture section. If you are pursuing 15-inch black crappie or 15-inch white crappie and the pictures do not show crappie of that length, then you may want to find another guide.

Once you select a guide, inform the guide about the size of fish you need to catch. Many states have weight and length guidelines indicating what fish will qualify as a record. An honest guide or charter service will give you an idea whether you have a high probability of catching a certain sized fish in a specific area. Several guides have directed me to a competitor because they knew they could not obtain the fish needed for my record requirements.

Inform the guide you may measure and weigh a potential record fish and ask if there is an accurate measuring device or a certified scale available. If documentation equipment is unavailable, inform the guide you will be bringing your own. Notify the guide you may be releasing fish of a certain size or fishing with a specific technique such as a fly rod. The guide needs to know specific photographs are essential, and this may take time away from fishing. Convey that you must meet all the state, IGFA, or FFHF requirements for your record to be accepted. To comply with these rules, it is necessary to hook and fight a fish with no assistance from the guide. If the guide touches the rod or line your IGFA world record will be disqualified, and your state or FFHF record may be disqualified.

If guides and deckhands do not understand fish record requirements, they may want to hook a fish and hand you the rod potentially resulting in a lost record. Guides are often more proficient than their customers at hooking a specific species of fish. Therefore, fish may be lost when customers attempt to hook fish themselves. Guides typically do not like to lose fish. Some guides are inflexible and will not change the way they fish to meet your requirements. Remember to weigh all your options when choosing a guide.

A guide's income is dependent on a client's fishing experience, and the ability to catch fish is important in maintaining a guide's reputation. For advertisement purposes, guides desire to display pictures of big fish to show off their expertise. A knowledgeable guide may be your best chance at catching a record size fish. A potential dilemma may arise if a guide is inflexible and will not allow you to use a specific technique while fishing. If their inflexibility eliminates your chance of catching a record under the required rules, then find another guide.

Be kind to your guide. As a general rule, you should always strive to treat others with respect. Remember your guide can control the outcome of your day. If your guide has an enjoyable trip, typically you will end the day with more fish. Most guides indicate they treat all guests equally. Many times this is not the case. Reputable guides will try to achieve a standard of fairness but may extend a fishing trip if they are having a good time with their guests. It is difficult for anyone to have a pleasurable experience when dealing with rude, drunk, or unruly patrons.

Generally, your guide will create several opportunities throughout the day where turning the boat one way will result in the best chance you may ever have to catch a record fish, or the guide can turn the boat the other way, and you will have a fairly good chance of catching a record fish. Be nice to your guide.

If you have the ability, provide a generous tip. Besides being appropriate, a large tip may pay off on your next trip. Do not base the tip on the size or quantity of fish you catch. Sometimes fish bite, and sometimes they do not.

Base the tip on the effort put forth by the guide and the willingness of the guide to help you catch a record. If your guide is disrespectful, do not tip and do not go back. However before affecting your guide's income, remember guides are human, and your guide may just be having a bad day. My wife is not very forgiving on this issue. She has pointed out on more than one occasion that she is not paying for someone to yell at her even if she makes mistakes resulting in lost fish or if her errors cause a guide to sacrifice a specific agenda.

On one guided trip, the guide said the fishing was so slow that he did not want us to pay for the trip. Both of us felt the trip was great even with slow fishing. The guide was enthusiastic the entire day, so I forced him to take the money for the trip. He said he would take the payment if he could take us again at a discounted rate. Agreeing to his terms, on our next trip the captain worked hard again, and my state record and FFHF world record hybrid striped bass was the result. Because of his attitude and friendly nature, we have fished with this guide on many occasions. We also recommend his guide services to other anglers. Fishing with guides can pay off with records.

It amazes me that many guides do not become educated about available record programs and explain these programs to their clients. Some anglers would pay extra if they knew they had a chance to post a record catch on a fishing trip. If guides were aware of record programs and requirements, they could charge a fee for filing the required documentation to achieve a record.

Seasonal programs are also fantastic to promote. New York has an annual recognition program, so a client has a chance at a record fish every year. Texas has a big fish award and elite angler award program where every angler can achieve this recognition independently. These types of programs are valuable to a guide since one client does not replace the award of another client. Pursuing multi-species records can result in anglers returning for guided fishing trips on a regular basis until all the desired species are caught.

- UNIQUE SPECIES -

The morning of fly fishing was excellent. I landed several common carp and a few channel catfish. It was a cool sunny morning, and the water quality improved from the muddied conditions brought by the spring floods. There were several common carp feeding around floating debris near the water's edge. The floating elk hair fly landed a few inches in front of a common carp just after it made a swirl in the water. Suddenly a bright orange fish came up through the water and grabbed the fly. The hook set felt good, and the fight was on. Working the fish up to the shore revealed that my hook was lodged in a large goldfish. Hundreds of fish had been hooked in this large public reservoir, but this was definitely a unique species for the lake.

Grabbing the net to land the goldfish, my expectations sank as the fish dislodged the hook and escaped. Was this another record lost? Examining the state record list, to my surprise, there was already a state rod and reel record, a state fly rod record, and even a waterbody record for goldfish. My fish would not have surpassed the state rod and reel record, but it would have been large enough to replace the state fly rod record. Another unique record lost.

Certain states limit records to common or native fish found within the state, while others do not exclude introduced or unique species. Goldfish, oscars, suckermouth catfish, pacu, Nile tilapia, and other introduced species may be potential records. During my electroshocking sampling of irrigation canals in Arizona to determine the diversity of fish populations, it was obvious that there is an excellent chance of encountering a unique species in warm climates. Some anglers might consider holding a record lionfish as a lesser award, but like my IGFA all-tackle world record gulf toadfish, the award maintains an honored location on my wall. Records are a valuable form of achievement no matter the size of the fish. Catching unique species is also an exhilarating experience.

Do not dismiss hard to catch unusual species when striving for records. This is especially true when fishing in saltwater. My wife is an expert at catching weird, unusual, strange, and unique species. She has landed sand tilefish, hairy blenny, scrawled filefish, doctorfish, pearly razorfish, and even a 12-inch mantis shrimp on a rod and reel. Many anglers land unusual fish that are small in size and do not know that these adult fish have record potential. Even after landing a state or world record fish, often an angler simply releases the fish before realizing a record was caught. Some organizations, including the FFHF and BAA, provide records for variations of fish species such

142 | THE ART OF FISHING FOR RECORDS

Check the record books if you land a unique species. This unusual 16-inch, 2.79-pound hybrid tilapia resulted in a waterbody record.

as mirror carp and koi, even though these fish are the same species as common carp (*Cyprinus carpio*). Check documented records before you release an unusual species to determine if a record is available.

- MULTIPLE RODS -

The June morning sun appeared over the horizon, and although channel catfish and largemouth bass were caught with the Plnor method, my smallmouth bass goal eluded me. My mission was to set a state record using the Plnor method, and the category for pole and line was vacant for smallmouth bass. Therefore, a smallmouth bass over half a pound would result in a state record.

Normally only one or two rods are used for Plnor fishing since the line is wrapped around a spool lying on the ground or placed in a bucket. Using more than one rod can result in the potential for massive tangles. Since fishing was slow, two rods were used most of the day and then a third rod was later added.

The middle rod lunged forward and bent over. Grabbing the rod, a 26-inch channel catfish was pulled to the shore. Just as the channel catfish was returned to the water, a second rod bent over. Fortunately, the line from the first rod was already out of the way as the second fish hooked-up. After reaching for the second rod, the fight was on. The Mustad hook worked well as the fish became tangled in submerged vegetation. Finally, the fish appeared near the surface, and the dark green color of the smallmouth bass was clearly visible. My excitement built realizing that landing the fish would result in a state record.

The fish was netted. My relief while landing the smallmouth bass was interrupted by my third rod bending over hard. Flipping the net over to trap the smallmouth bass, I stood on the net with the fish in the water. Lifting the other rod to set the hook resulted in a largemouth bass rocketing into the air. The fish jumped repeatedly throwing its head back and forth trying to dislodge the hook, and headed for a swim platform floating in the lake. My fingers burned as the line passed through them in short bursts. Stripping line back through the guides only took a few minutes as the largemouth bass was brought near the shore. Carefully picking up and opening the net at my feet, the exhausted largemouth bass swam into the net alongside the smallmouth bass. Raising the net, I realized it contained not one but two state records in the unrestricted other methods category. Both records were submitted, and in a few weeks, both state record certificates arrived in the mail from the Texas Parks and Wildlife Department.

Fishing with more than one or two rods is illegal in some situations, so check regulations before fishing with multiple rods. Fishing with more than one rod is common for many anglers, but fishing with a large number of rods at the same time is atypical. Six to ten personal rods are usually rigged on my fishing expeditions, and six or seven of them are used simultaneously when fishing is slow. On one of my guided catfish trips, the guide used eleven rods. He indicated that using multiple rods was one of the most important techniques he applied to stay in business by providing his clients with a high probability of success. His boat looked like an enormous spider with rods suspended in all directions.

The disadvantage of using multiple rods includes the cost of the equipment and the time it takes to rig them. Multiple rods can result in tangled lines and lost fish. If fishing is fast and furious, you may not be able to put out more than one or two rods before fighting a fish. Multiple rods work best when the action is slow to moderate and provides more opportunities for fish to find your bait. Rigging rods with different baits increases your chances of catching various species. If you are really ambitious, you can cast a lure or a fly while waiting for fish to bite your baited rods. It is truly a matter of working the percentages to hook more potential records.

One secret to fishing with multiple rods is to keep your lines tight by using slightly heavier weights or by trolling at a very slow speed. You will have fewer tangles when fighting fish next to tight lines as opposed to slack lines. You need patience when a hooked fish tangles all your lines creating an hour of work to re-rig. In one case, five fish were hooked up at once, and landing four of the five was a major success even after taking into account the hour needed to untangle all the lines once the excitement subsided.

SECRETS TO SUCCESS | 145

Barry Osborn's smallmouth bass and largemouth bass are both unrestricted Texas state records caught consecutively and netted together using the Plnor method.

Expect the unexpected while fishing and learn to be flexible and patient. Seeking a world record using multiple lines can be a gamble. An IGFA world record is disqualified if fighting the fish results in the fish becoming entangled on another line. Be mindful when selecting the number of rods to use when pursuing an IGFA world record. In certain circumstances, it is better to fish with fewer rods.

7

MIND GAMES

- ENJOY FISHING -

It was a dusty walk down the red dirt Oklahoma cow path to a small upland pond. My grandfather "Buster" was in the lead followed by my high school sweetheart and future bride, Karen. We were all expecting an exciting day of fishing. It was a beautiful morning with puffy clouds dotting a blue sky. My trusty fiberglass rod mounted with a Zebco 33 reel bounced with each step. In my other hand, Buster's old galvanized bucket full of minnows splashed droplets of water on the ground with each swing.

We reached the water's edge and baited our hooks. The wind was mild, and Karen's red and white bobber made a plopping sound as it entered the water near the cattails. The bobber floated slowly then began to bounce frantically before disappearing under the water. Karen tightened her line, set the hook, and the fight was on. After a few minutes had passed, she landed a largemouth bass. It was a nice fat four pounder, but Buster and I celebrated like it was a 14-pound ShareLunker. At the time, Karen and I did not realize this was the start of a fishing relationship that would last us a lifetime.

Throughout the day, we landed several more largemouth bass, channel catfish, white crappie, and bluegill. Our fishing equipment was not expensive, and we did not have a boat. The trip was spontaneous with little planning involved. The fish were not large, and none

Fishing can result in years of family enjoyment. Karen Osborn and Alvin "Buster" Jackson, Barry Osborn's grandfather, are featured with large stringers of sunfish in 1979.

of them would be listed as records, but the day was filled with smiles, hugs, jokes, and stories from past adventures. It was a perfect day.

Decades later, on another fishing excursion, Karen was fishing beside me as my Penn International reel clicked a few times as the line was gently pulled from the reel. A few seconds later, the rod doubled over as an eight-foot-long shortfin mako shark rocketed into the air creating a huge splash as the fish reentered the water. My fight with the approximately 300-pound shark lasted for over an hour. There were eleven jumps in all before the mako pulled the hook. The fight did not result in any records, and this trip was extremely different from the day of pond fishing with my wife and grandfather years before. Still, the day provided another great memory that will forever be etched in my mind. Fish often and enjoy every moment.

Angling takes many forms. Over the decades, the hundreds of days spent fishing have been some of the best days of my life. Countless memories fishing with family and friends will stay with me throughout my remaining years. Lord willing, there will be many more happy and invigorating days of fishing ahead. Not every trip will result in records. Documenting information to obtain records can result in unwanted complexities and serve as a distraction from fishing fun. Do not let record data collection ruin the enjoyment of a fishing trip. Fishing records are similar to photographs and videos. Time is needed to create them, but your efforts can provide a physical reminder of a cherished fishing day. Therefore, ensure prized memories are not tarnished in the midst of the hard work needed to fulfill your goals. Precious time with others is one of the greatest success stories any angler can achieve.

Make fishing engaging and fun for rookie anglers. Begin fishing for a species that is readily available and will provide fast action. Although a young angler will be proud to obtain a first fish award, the junior angler will not enjoy the experience if there is undesirable pressure to achieve the award. An earthworm, shrimp, or squid on a hook is usually the best way to get a fish on the line depending on whether you are fishing in freshwater or saltwater. Do not overstay while fishing with a beginner or with any angler for that matter. This

Take time to teach young anglers how to fish, including the importance of following the rules and regulations. The Mosley family including Laura, Alexis, Doug, and Braxton is shown admiring Braxton's common carp.

is definitely a challenge for me, and I have exacerbated an angler on more than one occasion. It is always better to end a fishing trip at a time when fellow anglers will leave wanting more instead of staying until they want to go home.

Realize that not every angler will be excited about your endeavors to learn the art of fishing for records and may not be interested in documenting record fish. Some anglers believe time spent documenting a record takes away from the fishing experience. Everyone is entitled to an opinion, so do not let the opinions of others take away from your enthusiasm concerning records.

We are blessed to have fishing opportunities available throughout our nation. Appreciate the satisfaction of every fish that ends up on your hook. If you only enjoy fish resulting in a record catch, you will miss out on ninety-nine percent of the experience. Take time to pay attention to the world around you while fishing. Do not let the intensity of pursuing a record cause you to miss a family of raccoons fishing on the bank. Do not miss the smile on your child's face or the grin of a friend during a fun fishing adventure. Our world is full of stress, pressure, and complications. Take time to slow down and relish the thrill of every tug on your line.

- ETHICS -

There was a chill in the air as the white streamer fly landed near the edge of the dock. Stripping the line through the fly rod had yet to produce results. It was February, and the fish were feeding slowly. The next cast was long, and after waiting a few seconds, it appeared as though the fly reached the bottom. A small strip of the line was interrupted by a hard strike, converting the calmness of the morning into a frenzied fight. The fish shot under a boat dock and tangled on a cable. By gently working the fish, it finally came free and headed toward deeper water. After several seconds, the noteworthy white crappie was slowly pulled into the net. A plastic measuring tape was used to take a rough measurement along the contour of the fish's body indicating the fish was just less than 16 inches in length.

My excitement was building. To qualify for a big fish award in Texas, white crappie must be at least 15 inches in total length and measured on a flat surface with their mouths closed. Utilizing this method, a fish can be manipulated and its fins moved to obtain the maximum length, but the measurement cannot be taken along the contour of the fish or with the fish's mouth open.

The white crappie was placed in a bucket of water and carried to a measuring board. It measured 14.75 inches in total length. After moving and adjusting the fish every way possible, it was clear the 15-inch length could not be legitimately obtained. This white crappie could have been an important fish for me. To qualify for the Texas Parks and Wildlife Freshwater Elite Angler Award, an angler needs five different big freshwater fish species of a minimum size. It can take a lifetime to achieve this award, and with two big fish awards already obtained, another big fish would move me closer toward my goal.

While standing on the dock, a series of thoughts quickly ran through my mind, "The fish is only one-quarter of an inch off the mark. Who is going to know if the fish is reported to be 15 inches in length? The fish can easily be moved 0.25 inches down the board, and nobody will ever know." Fortunately, after coming to my senses, the thought, "I will know" entered my mind. Why taint this record and my eventual freshwater elite angler award by cheating.

I already possessed the white crappie fly fishing waterbody record, and although this fish could easily defeat the existing rod and reel waterbody record by weight, the catch occurred before the purchase of my personal certified scales. The long drive to reach the scales would require me to kill the magnificent fish just to get another lake record. I placed the fish in the lake and moved it gently back and forth to pass water over its gills. The white crappie revived and shook its head before disappearing into the green water.

The moral of the story is not to fib, exaggerate, lie, or cheat concerning a record. The simple act of taking a sloppy measurement or incorrectly rounding numbers can create a bad situation. Several documented records indicate a fish was measured inaccurately or a fish species was misidentified. In some cases, the weight or measurement

Karen Osborn is holding a 13.5-inch black crappie weighing 1.33 pounds. Accurately measuring, weighing, and identifying the fish allowed her to receive a waterbody record.

of a documented fish is clearly incorrect, raising concern about the ethics of the angler who submitted the record, along with the official who certified it. This is a reason why the IGFA and other organizations are so meticulous about reviewing record submittals.

Unfortunately, I have spoken with anglers who have lied about their records. Most of these anglers feel remorse about the records they falsified and wish they could go back and remove them. One angler with multiple records indicated, "I am really proud of my state record because I caught it totally by myself and completely within the rules." It would be better if he could say that about all of his records.

If an angler deliberately falsifies a record, several states have clauses calling for the removal of all the angler's records and may disallow the angler to submit records in the future. For big tournaments with cash rewards fish may be x-rayed to prevent cheating, and there can be criminal charges associated with falsifying catch information. The most important reason to avoid cheating is so a record will not incur a negative meaning. Prized records are meant to instill a feeling of joy and satisfaction in an angler, not a feeling of shame.

Honesty is especially important for children and young adults. Do not put them in a position where they feel they cheated to receive a record. The whole purpose of recognition is to create a situation an angler can be proud of. Cheating and lying diminishes your character and steals from the legitimate record holder you replace.

- THE DARK SIDE -

It would be wonderful if all of your fishing trips were fun and calm with birds chirping, the sun shining, fish jumping in the boat, and smiles all around. However we are human, and emotions can escalate during the heat of a fishing battle. Keep your desire to learn the art of fishing for records from adversely affecting the fun, relationships, and happiness of a fishing event. Although my wife loves to fish, she has not been interested in setting records. She is a carefree person and enjoys fishing for the time outdoors and the camaraderie that ensues with friends and family, until recently.

One day while we were looking at my saltwater elite angler award, Karen said she would like to have one of her own. In fact, Karen decided she wanted both a freshwater and saltwater elite angler award. We discussed the time and work it had taken me to get the ten big fish of different species needed to achieve both awards. Karen indicated she was up for the challenge especially since completing the task would make her the first woman in Texas to receive both elite angler awards. Since we enjoy fishing together, we began planning and booked some trips. Due to work and other commitments, we wanted to maximize our chances of getting a big saltwater fish. King mackerel appeared to be Karen's best chance at acquiring a quick big fish award, so we booked a trip on a charter party boat.

We informed the deckhand concerning our desire to catch records including Karen's quest for a 40-inch king mackerel to go toward her saltwater elite angler award. The deckhand indicated that king mackerel were actively biting and getting Karen a 40-inch fish should not be a problem. We did not know at the time that this was going to be one of the most unlucky days to attain a record we had ever seen.

Most of the anglers were fishing on the bottom for red snapper. Karen already had a big fish award for red snapper, and we rigged some flat lines and drifted them behind the boat for king mackerel. Our first priority was for Karen to catch the big king mackerel she needed toward her saltwater elite angler award, then work on adding other big fish award species if possible. My goal was to catch a state record fish while using the Plnor fishing method.

Our two personal rods were baited with scaled sardines and were drifting behind the boat. To increase Karen's chances, the deckhand put out boat rods rigged for king mackerel. This is a common practice on a party boat, and any angler in the vicinity is allowed to grab one of these rods if a fish takes the bait. We waited expectantly.

The first fish bite occurred on one of my rods, and the fish stripped line off the reel with lightning speed. Karen quickly headed toward the rod. She removed it from the holder and skillfully fought the fish to the gaff. The deckhand made a difficult gaff and pulled the fish on board. The thought, "Well, that was easy!" went through my mind as the fish hit the deck. We put the king mackerel on a measuring board, and it measured 39.5 inches long. It was only one half inch short of the size Karen needed for her award. I thought to myself, "No problem, there is plenty of daylight left, and the fish are biting."

The next fish slammed a sardine and made a crazy long run. Karen fought the fish to the boat, and we could tell it was well over 40 inches in length. The deckhand started to gaff the king mackerel when it suddenly pulled free and swam away. Karen brought in the rig, and the hook was broken, not bent but broken. Another fish was lost with no fault on Karen's part.

Amazingly, this scenario continued over the next six hours. The next two fish Karen landed were less than one inch short of the required length. Throughout the day, Karen lost 8 large king mackerel near the boat, and none of these losses were her fault. Most of the king mackerel appeared to be large enough for a big fish award, but tangled lines, freak jumps, thrown hooks, and missed gaffs prevented a single 40-inch fish from hitting the deck.

My day was spent untangling lines, baiting hooks, and rigging Karen's line over and over without landing a single fish of my own. My frustration showed. The deckhand was also frustrated with all the freak situations. The trip was close to concluding when one of the rods bent over hard with line rapidly screaming off the reel. It was one of the deckhand's rods, and I told Karen to hurry and grab it quickly. She was finishing reeling in her rod, so she moved a few feet away to place her rod in a holder.

The deckhand grabbed the rod with the fish and gave it to a very old lady angler who decided she wanted to try and catch a big fish. His action was totally appropriate for the situation. The lady began reeling in the fish. The fish was hooked through the gills and was bleeding as it swam over to the boat, turned on its side, and allowed the deckhand to easily gaff it behind its head. He pulled the catch over the side and dropped the 42-inch king mackerel on the deck.

I could not believe that after hours of fishing Karen did not catch this fish. After the fish was on the deck, Karen could tell I was mad. I walked over to her and said, "Why didn't you grab the rod?" She said she was trying to, but she had to put her rod down before she could grab the other rod. Although that was the fact, my response was that she should have moved faster. Then she said, "I did my best." Her response made me even more upset. I thought, "Did her best… nobody ever really does their best. I could have easily gotten there faster!" The reality was someone was acting like an out of control child and that someone was me. At the time, I did not realize the stupidity of my position. The captain called over the radio and told us to pull in our lines. Fishing was over. We headed in, and Karen sat next to me and gently placed her hand on my knee. I was puffed up like a porcupinefish. Karen did not want to disappoint me, and by looking over at her, I could see there was a tear in the corner of her eye.

Immediately a different disposition came over me. The day without a fish for me and the lost record fish for Karen were now irrelevant. My reaction was clearly unjustified, and there was no reason to feel sorry for myself. I had agreed to donate time to help Karen achieve fishing records, and she had already invested time to help me. We had shared a beautiful day of fishing in calm seas, and Karen had caught multiple king mackerel. The day should have ended with happy memories. Instead, we were both upset, and it was my fault. My wife was hurt by my reaction over losing a stupid fish. I apologized. She accepted my apology, but the damage had been done. The dark mood of the day rested squarely on my shoulders.

Unfortunately, this is not the only instance when my response has been inappropriate while fishing. There are other occasions when fishing situations got under my skin. I am usually intense about most of the things I do. I like to set records. I like to win. I typically do not play games for the fun of it. I plan and invest my energy to accomplish my objectives. I am focused on the goal of the day and forget there are other viewpoints regarding fishing. Usually, my intensity does not interfere with the enjoyment of the sport, but sometimes I need to keep my attitude in check.

After an evening of trying to recover the fun we had lost, we were both feeling better. We decided to stay another night and try the next day for Karen's king mackerel big fish award. It was a weekday, and unlike the day before, there was an opening on a boat going out of Dolphin Docks in Port Aransas, Texas. We were hoping for success, and we booked an eight-hour trip.

We arrived at the first location to begin fishing, and after anchoring Captain Tim came down from his cabin to help the deckhands assist the anglers. Captain Tim is always friendly, and he was happy to see we were able to fish with them that day. Fishing with Dolphin Docks out of Port Aransas, Texas provides wonderful experiences, and the crew makes every effort to ensure all anglers are having a good time and catching a boatload of fish.

My personal rod baited with a sardine was already in the water. Captain Tim came over with a boat rod in hand. We informed the captain Karen was interested in catching a 40-inch king mackerel. He asked if she needed a 40-inch fish or a 40-pound fish. We told him about our exploits from the day before and indicated that the record we were after was based on length not weight, so we only needed a 40-inch fish measured by total length.

The captain informed us that was doable and cast out a rod with a sardine. He set the rod in the holder and barely removed his hand when the rod bent over hard. Karen pushed past me and grabbed the rod. Captain Tim smiled as he watched her fight the fish. It was a long hard fight. A deckhand moved other anglers out of the way allowing Karen to go over and under their rods as she fought the fish up and down the boat. The king mackerel was close to the gaff several times but then quickly swam away. Although king mackerel usually only deliver one big run, this fish never gave up. Finally, Karen reeled the king mackerel close enough for the deckhand to gaff it.

The deckhand pulled the fish over the side, and the 55-inch king mackerel hit the deck with a thud. This fish was a substantial catch and was well over the 40-inch length that Karen needed for her award. It was a magnificent fish, and the longest fish caught on the boat that day. Karen obtained her big fish award and added another fish to her saltwater elite angler award qualification. This event only reinforced the fact that my traumatic reaction from the day before was unwarranted and a complete waste of time.

MIND GAMES | 159

Maintain a positive attitude to keep fishing fun
and engaging. Karen Osborn's king mackerel
dwarfs Barry Osborn's fish…again.

Always be aware of the dark side of fishing. If you have a strong personality, you must actively evaluate each situation to keep from letting undesirable emotions override the fun and excitement of fishing. Fishing requires planning, expense, and energy. If you fish, there will be blood (often yours), bad weather, fishless days, tangled lines, broken rods, rods and reels dropped over the side, broken boats, flat tires, sea-sickness, pain, injuries, and upset anglers. Do not let these circumstances destroy the pleasure of a fishing trip. This is especially important for young or inexperienced anglers. Anglers will make mistakes, but making mistakes is how we all learn to fish.

To this day, reeling in my last line on a trip causes anxiety, especially on days when work is pending on the horizon. Having another fishing trip planned helps reduce anxiety, but leaving a fishing location is never enjoyable. Learn to soak in the treasured moments of your fishing experiences and dream of future records to be won.

8

A FINAL NOTE

Red, orange, and purple colors filled the sky as the sun disappeared below the horizon. It was a wonderful evening. Ripples moved across the smooth bay as the final remains of a red snapper landed in the water. Placing the last filet in a bowl concluded our fantastic day of offshore blue water fishing. Picking up the bowl of filets, my mind returned to the smile on Ken's face as he was holding up the big cobia he landed earlier. Heading up the stairs for a fresh fish meal with family and friends was a perfect end to a great day.

Respect other anglers. On more than one occasion anglers have called my records "paper records" or "cheap records." I have been called a liar, or worse, on several occasions both in person and on social media when discussing the numerous state records I have accumulated. Once, after discussing my active state records with a group of anglers, one angler harshly remarked, "You are full of crap." He then said, "Nobody can have over 50 state records. There aren't even that many state records available in Texas." Unfortunately, all the commenter needed to do was to visit the state's webpage to confirm these records for himself and see that there are hundreds of state records available when all species and categories are considered.

Other anglers have accused me of cheating on my records because they did not understand the method of fishing being applied or the record category involved to obtain my records. Once while fishing with a fly rod without a reel, I put bait on the fly. A deckhand told another angler I was cheating to acquire a fly fishing record. If I had turned in a fly fishing record, he would have been correct since bait is not allowed when submitting this type of record. In reality, I was not trying to acquire a fly fishing record. I was utilizing the Plnor fishing method. In Texas, by using the Plnor method, an angler can receive a legitimate pole and line no reel record in the other methods category using a baited fly.

Although baiting a fly will remove the chance for a fly fishing record, in some situations, you can still obtain a rod and reel record with a baited fly. There are several record options available depending on an organization's rules and the record category you are after. It may be appropriate to respectfully question an angler concerning their records, but make sure you know the facts before you accuse an angler of committing an inappropriate act.

Anglers often have varying viewpoints concerning the sport of fishing. Some anglers are seeking time away to relax, while others delight in a battle or a chance at winning a tournament. Unfortunately, I have seen fly fishing anglers cut down bait anglers, and largemouth bass anglers denigrate catfish anglers. Sadly, these anglers were not just joking around. This negative behavior adversely affects the spirit of camaraderie and the sport of fishing as a whole.

One evening while fishing on a bank, a young fisherman standing near me was extremely excited as he hooked a 29-inch common carp on a fly. He had observed me fly fishing, and I showed him how to fish using my fly rod. This was his first big fish on a fly. The fish was in superb condition and put up a fantastic fight. The common carp went well into the backing multiple times, and the angler did an amazing job bringing the fish to the net.

He was outwardly proud of his achievement until a bystander realized the fish was a common carp and said, "Oh it's just a trash fish." The bystander probably had never landed a fish anywhere close to 29 inches on a fly rod, but he considered himself knowledgeable enough to disrespect another angler's experience. Instead of tearing someone down, always strive to provide an encouraging word to brighten and uplift a fellow angler's day.

A FINAL NOTE | 163

Discover the beauty around you. Majestic scenery is part of the fishing experience.

Take time to teach others to fish. Our society is losing the fight to appreciate wildlife and the outdoors. An inquisitive youngster, who is constantly chatting while you are trying to catch a record fish, may be a reflection of how you once acted during your childhood. Do not discourage junior anglers. Answer their questions. Teach them how to tie a knot that will withstand the fight of a record fish, and show them how to properly bait a hook. Teaching new anglers will ultimately increase the number of fishing enthusiasts, leading to expanded efforts to protect the resource and benefit future generations.

In our fast-paced, high-tech world, do not let the challenge, excitement, and thrill of fishing pass you by. Although it is often difficult to find time to get away, fishing opportunities abound in our great nation. Thousands of fish are caught every year by anglers sitting beneath a highway bridge in a congested, energetic city.

Aesthetically, fishing in a city may not compare to a trip in the Florida Keys or a hike to a mountain stream, but these types of outings still provide outstanding opportunities to relax and soak in the wonder of the outdoors. The beauty of fishing is that it does not discriminate. Fishing provides pleasure to all anglers from different backgrounds and various cultures. An exciting catch brings joy to a wealthy participant on a yacht in the same way it does to a small child, with limited means, standing along the bank of a lake or ocean. Anyone can master the art of fishing for records.

Protect and conserve the resource. Strive to understand the environmental consequences of fishing. There are varying viewpoints concerning the impacts fishing can have on a fish population. Ensure your angling activities do not adversely affect the aquatic resource. Understanding the art of fishing for records improves the sport of fishing by increasing interest and redirecting money toward expanded fishing opportunities. These efforts will ultimately lead to further protection of the aquatic environment.

Our oceans, rivers, streams, lakes, ponds, wetlands, and marshes are our legacy to our children. Remember to remove empty containers and do not pollute the area where you fish. Learn about endangered, threatened, and protected species and safeguard those individuals.

A FINAL NOTE | 165

Be respectful while fishing in environmentally sensitive areas. Rudy and Cindy Garza are trout fishing in Colorado at 13,000 feet.

Educate yourself concerning potentially invasive species and do not inadvertently spread these species to another waterbody. Both plant and animal invasive species are a serious problem in lakes and rivers throughout our nation. Study, observe, and comply with all fishing regulations to conserve the fishing resource. These efforts are a major aspect of learning the art of fishing for records.

You must go fishing to catch fishing records. This is a straightforward idea, but taking time out of your schedule to fish is the first step to acquire records. With all of the tournaments, clubs, organizations, state programs, world record programs, and multi-species awards available, there are endless opportunities to achieve records, awards, and recognition. The art of fishing for records is a process where you can attain a goal while creating a canvas for others to share and enjoy. Learning the art of fishing for records is an exciting endeavor, and mastering new methods will take time, energy, and practice. Have fun every time your hook hits the water because your next cast could be the one that results in a new record fish. See you on the water.

OSBORN OVERKILL KNOT

The Osborn Overkill Knot is a combination knot I created to catch record fish including multiple state and world records. Although the knot looks elaborate, and seems complicated at first, through practice, it is relatively easy to master. Three braided lengths of line above the terminal tackle make the knot extremely durable.

The Osborn Overkill Knot is tied in three different steps using monofilament, fluorocarbon, or braided line and can be attached to a hook, snap, leader, lure, or other terminal tackle. Although the knot has disadvantages including the fact that it takes time to tie, is more visible than a smaller knot, and is difficult to pull tight using monofilament line that is over 130-pound test, the advantages greatly outweigh the disadvantages. The knot is very strong. If a snag occurs, an angler's fishing line will typically break at a weak point between the knot and the rod tip. This may result in the loss of a large quantity of line, but an angler will notice the knot will usually stay intact.

The durability of the knot aids in preventing an angler from losing record fish. It is abrasion resistant since line goes through the terminal tackle three times and helps protect an angler's fishing line an inch or two above the knot. The knot creates a shock absorber effect in the line to stop it from breaking and to keep a hook from pulling out of a fish. An angler can see this effect in action by holding the terminal tackle and pulling on the knot. Visit osbornfishing.com, youtube, or continue reading to see how to tie the knot yourself.

168 | THE ART OF FISHING FOR RECORDS

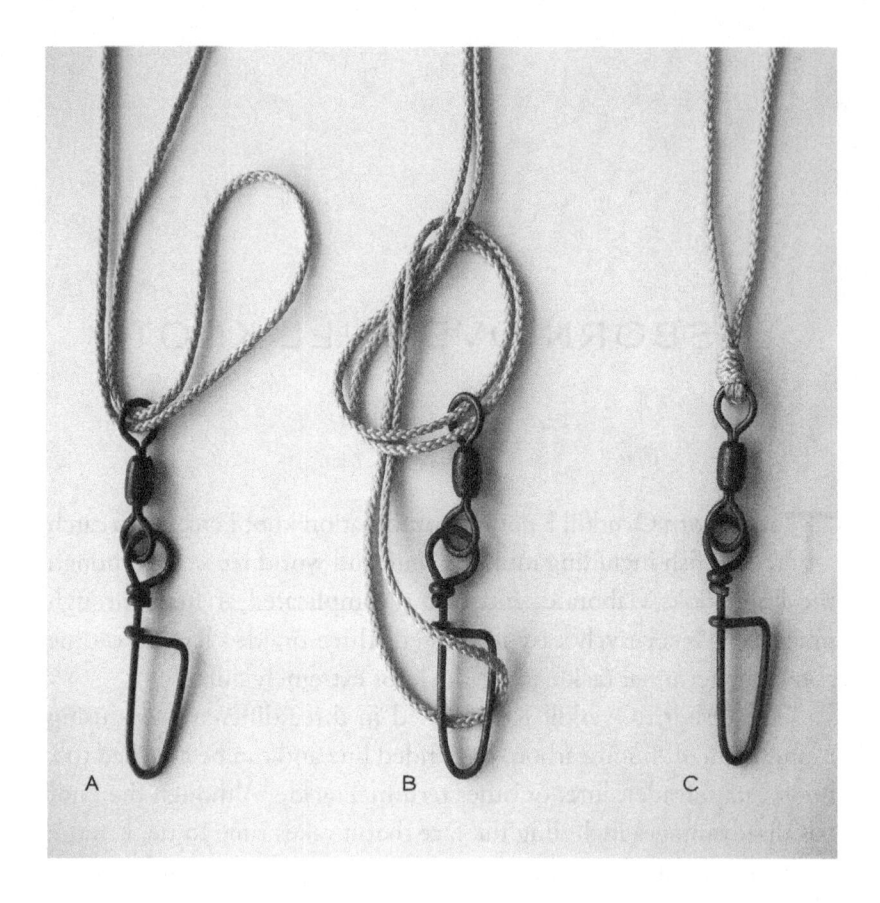

Step one is to double the line and pass the doubled line through the swivel on the snap creating a loop and long tag end (A). Take the loop and tie an overhand loop over the main line and tag end (B). Pass the snap through the loop and pull tight (C).

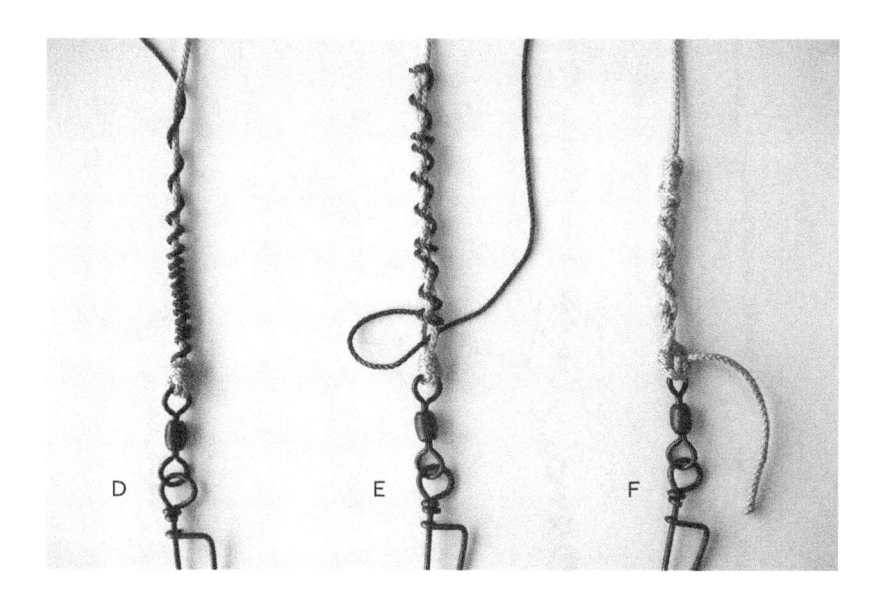

Step two is the process of completing the main twists of the knot. For clarification, another color line was spliced onto the tag end to show the active part of the knot. Hold the knot tied in step one, and pull the main line tight against the rod. Take the tag end of the line and twist it up the main line 15 times toward the rod (D).

When you complete the 15 twists, with the line still tight, bring the tag end back away from the rod toward the swivel, and the line will begin wrapping back over the twists you have just made. It's like magic. Wrap back down over the earlier twists 9 to 11 times until you reach the two lines in front of the overhand knot on the swivel. Now you need to complete the challenging phase of the knot. Take the tag end of the line and pass it between the two lines in front of the overhand knot described in step one. You can carefully use a hook to separate the lines if needed to create an opening between the lines. Once you have the tag end through the lines, the knot is stable (E).

Now grab the tag end of the line and the main line, with the terminal tackle hanging, and pull steadily. If this step is completed correctly, the top of the knot will tighten and result in the appearance of two different types of wraps (F).

170 | THE ART OF FISHING FOR RECORDS

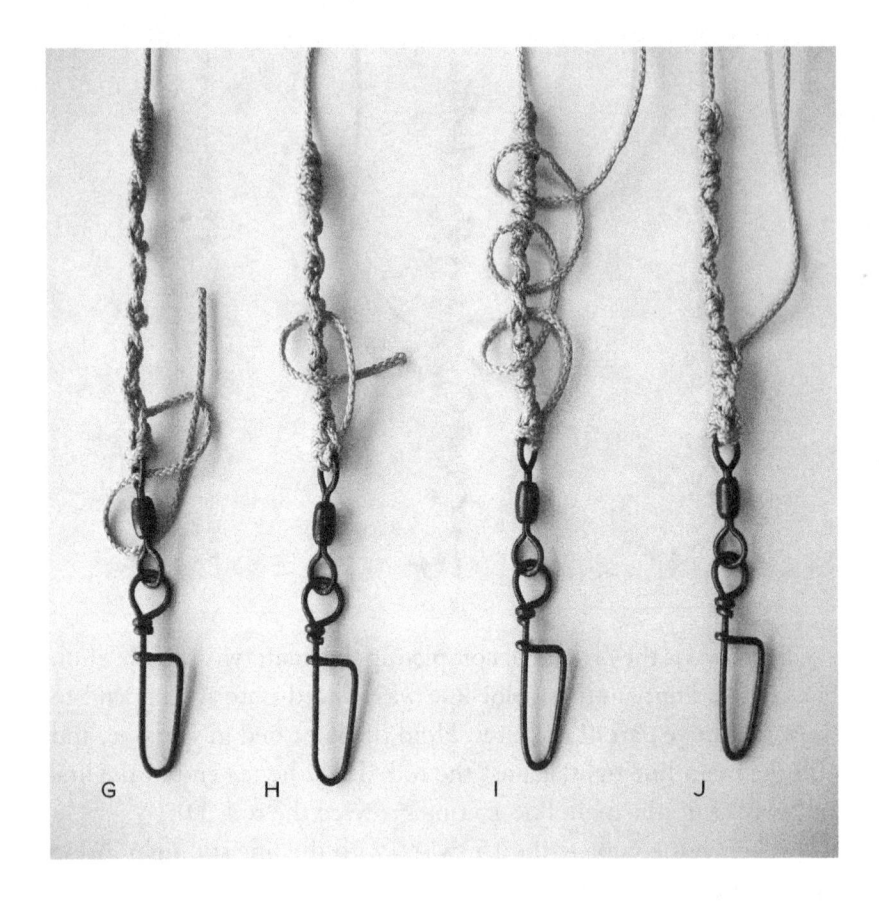

G　　　　H　　　　I　　　　J

Step three consists of five half hitches. Start by passing the tag end through the swivel, and then pass the tag end through the loop (half-hitch) you just created (G). Pull tight. Make a loop over the main line knot and pass the tag end through the loop (H).

Pull tight. Repeat this action three more times pulling the tag end tight between each half-hitch (I). The outcome should result in the tag end being perpendicular to the main line (J). Cut the tag end leaving a small amount of line. Your knot is now complete.

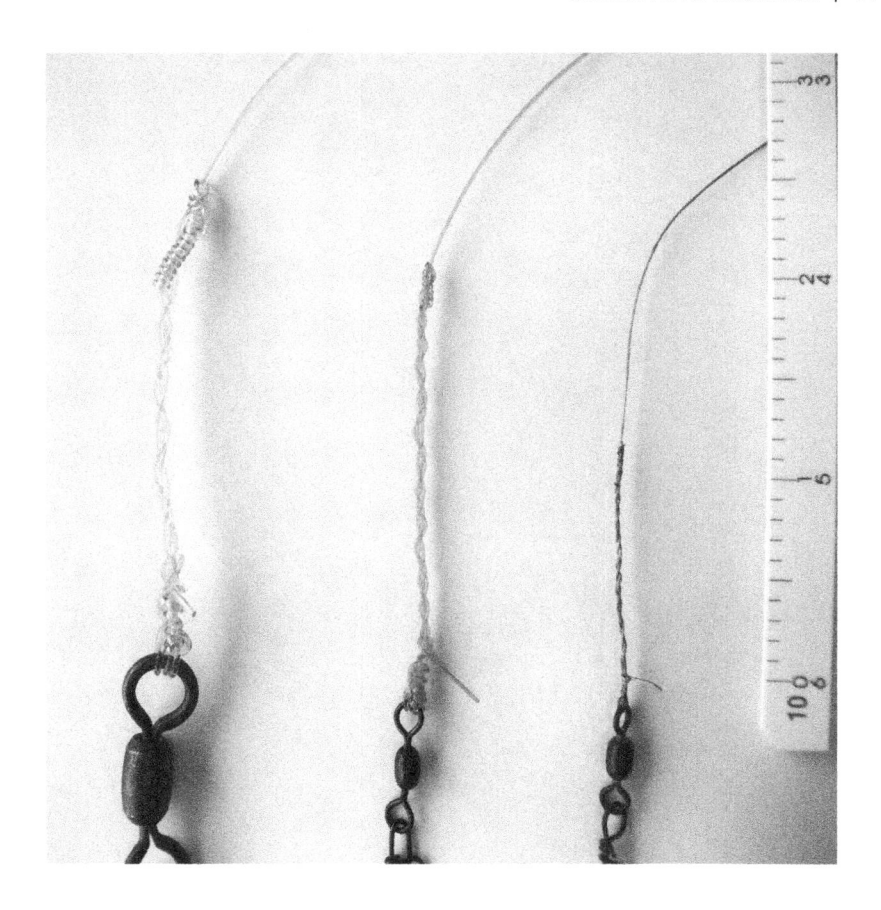

Utilizing monofilament, the finished Osborn Overkill Knot will be approximately two inches long. From left to right is 80-pound Berkley ProSpec line, 25-pound Berkley Big Game line, and 50-pound PowerPro braid line.

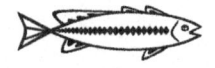

FISH NOMENCLATURE

Format of Nomenclature:

Common Name
Scientific Name
Local Name

Amberjack, Greater
Seriola dumerili
AJ, Jack, Reef Donkey

Anchovy, Striped
Anchoa hepsetus
Broad-striped Anchovy

Barracuda, Great
Sphyraena barracuda
Giant Barracuda, Cuda

Bass, Alabama
Micropterus henshalli
Alabama Spotted Bass

Bass, Hybrid Striped
Morone chrysops x M. saxatilis
Whiterock Bass, Palmeto Bass

Bass, Largemouth
Micropterus salmoides
Bigmouth Bass, Black Bass

Bass, Smallmouth
Micropterus dolomieu
Brown Bass, Bronze Bass

Bass, Striped
Morone saxatilis
Striper, Rockfish

Bass, White
Morone chrysops
Sand Bass, Silver Bass

Bass, Yellow
Morone mississippiensis
Yellow Striper

Blenny, Hairy
Labrisomus nuchipinnis
Fire Belly

Bluegill
Lepomis macrochirus
Sunfish, Brim, Bream, Perch

Bonnethead
Sphyrna tiburo
Bonnethead Shark, Shovelhead

Buffalo, Black
Ictiobus niger
Current Buffalo

Buffalo, Smallmouth
Ictiobus bubalus
Buff, Razorback, Bullfish

Carp, Common
Cyprinus carpio
European Carp

Catfish, Blue
Ictalurus furcatus
Silver Cat

Catfish, Channel
Ictalurus punctatus
Fork-tail Cat, Spotted Cat

Catfish, Flathead
Pylodictis olivaris
Opelousas Cat, Yellow Cat

Catfish, Gafftopsail
Bagre marinus
Gafftop, Sail Cat

Catfish, Hardhead
Ariopsis felis
Hardhead, Tourist Trout

Catfish, Suckermouth
Hypostomus plecostomus
Plecostomus, Armored Catfish

Cobia
Rachycentron canadum
Ling, Lemon Fish

Crappie, Black
Pomoxis nigromaculatus
Black Perch, Calico Bass, Slab

Crappie, White
Pomoxis annularis
White Perch, Pan Fish, Slab

Croaker, Atlantic
Micropogonias undulatus
Croaker

Croaker, White
Genyonemus lineatus
Croaker, Roncador, Tom Cod

Cutlassfish, Atlantic
Trichiurus lepturus
Largehead Hairtail, Ribbonfish

Doctorfish
Acanthurus chirurgus
Doctorfish Tang, Surgeonfish

Dolphin
Coryphaena hippurus
Mahi-Mahi, Dorado

Drum, Red
Sciaenops ocellatus
Redfish, Rat-red, Sea Bass

Drum, Freshwater
Aplodinotus grunniens
Gaspergou, Grinder

Filefish, Scrawled
Aluterus scriptus
Scribbled Leatherjacket Filefish

Flounder, Southern
Paralichthys lethostigma
Flounder, Flatfish, Doormat

Gar, Alligator
Atractosteus spatula
Gator Gar

Goldfish
Carassius auratus
Golden Carp, Comet

Grouper, Goliath
Epinephelus itajara
Atlantic Goliath G., Jewfish

Grouper, Red
Epinephelus morio
Brown Grouper, Hamlet

Grunt, White
Haemulon plumierii
White Snapper, Common Grunt

Jack, Almaco
Seriola rivoliana
Longfin Yellowtail, Bar Jack

Jack, Crevalle
Caranx hippos
Jackfish, Common Jack

Ladyfish
Elops saurus
Little Tarpon, Skipjack

Lingcod
Ophiodon elongatus
Buffalo Cod, Green Cod

Lionfish
Pterois volitans
Red Lionfish, Firefish

Lizardfish, Inshore
Synodus foetens
Lizardfish, Sand Pike

Mackerel, King
Scomberomorus cavalla
King, Kingfish

Mackerel, Spanish
Scomberomorus maculatus
Atlantic Spanish Mackerel

Mako, Shortfin
Isurus oxyrinchus
Mako, Mako Shark, Blue Pointer

Marlin, Blue
Makaira nigricans
Atlantic Blue Marlin, Billfish

Mullet, Striped
Mugil cephalus
Flathead Grey Mullet

Oscar
Astronotus ocellatus
Tiger Oscar, Red Oscar

Pacu
Colossoma macropomum
Cachama, Tambaqui, Black Pacu

Perch, Sand
Diplectrum formosum
Sand Seabass, Sandfish

Pinfish
Lagodon rhomboides
Perch, Piggy Perch

Porcupinefish
Diodon hystrix
Spot-fin Porcupinefish

Puffer, Smooth
Lagocephalus laevigatus
Puff, Spotted Puffer

Razorfish, Pearly
Xyrichtys novacula
Cleaver Wrasse

Remora
Remora remora
Shark Sucker, Brown Remora

Runner, Blue
Caranx crysos
Hardtail Jack, Hardnose

Sailfish
Istiophorus albicans
Atlantic Sailfish, Sail

Sardine, Scaled
Harengula jaguana
Scaled Herring, Sardine

Seatrout, Sand
Cynoscion arenarius
Sand Weakfish, Sand Trout

Seatrout, Spotted
Cynoscion nebulosus
Spotted Weakfish, Speck

Shad, Gizzard
Dorosoma cepedianum
American Gizzard Shad

Shad, Threadfin
Dorosoma petenense
Shad, Spotted Shad

Shark, Atlantic Sharpnose
Rhizoprionodon terraenovae
Bull Tiger Shark

Shark, Blacktip
Carcharhinus limbatus
Blackfin, Black-tipped Shark

Shark, Nurse
Ginglymostoma cirratum
Cat Shark

Shark, Spinner
Carcharhinus brevipinna
Great Blacktip Shark

Shark, Tiger
Galeocerdo cuvier
Maneater, Sea Tiger

Shark, Whale
Rhincodon typus
Basking Shark, Whaleshark

Sharksucker
Echeneis naucrates
Live Sharksucker, Remora

Sheepshead
Archosargus probatocephalus
Convict Fish

Snapper, Gray
Lutjanus griseus
Mangrove Snapper, Mango

Snapper, Mutton
Lutjanus analis
King Snapper

Snapper, Red
Lutjanus campechanus
Northern Red Snapper

Snapper, Vermilion
Rhomboplites aurorubens
B-liner

Snook, Common
Centropomus undecimalis
Robalo, Saltwater Pike

Stingray, Atlantic
Hypanus sabinus
Pointed Snout Stingray

Stingray, Bluntnose
Hypanus say
Say's Stingray

Stingray, Southern
Hypanus americanus
Stingaree

Sunfish, Green
Lepomis cyanellus
Greenie, Perch

Sunfish, Longear
Lepomis megalotis
Cherry Bream, Perch, Sunfish

Tarpon
Megalops atlanticus
Silver King

Tilapia, Blue
Oreochromis aureus
Tilapia, Blue Perch

Tilapia, Nile
Oreochromis niloticus
Tilapia, Nile Perch

Tilefish, Sand
Malacanthus plumieri
Sandfish

Toadfish, Gulf
Opsanus beta
Dogfish, Oysterfish, Rockfish

Triggerfish, Gray
Balistes capriscus
Grey Triggerfish

Trout, Cutthroat
Oncorhynchus clarkii
Harvest Trout

Trout, Rainbow
Oncorhynchus mykiss
Bow

Tuna, Blackfin
Thunnus atlanticus
Blackfin, Albacore

Tuna, Yellowfin
Thunnus albacares
Yellowfin, Longfin Tuna

Tunny, Little
Euthynnus alletteratus
Bonito, False Albacore

Wahoo
Acanthocybium solandri
Ono, Hoo, Speedster

Walleye
Sander vitreus
Walleyed Perch, Pikeperch

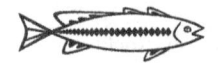

INDEX

Alabama bass, 59
alligator gar, 77
all-tackle world record, 2, 6, 141
almaco jack, 22, 58, 114
Ambassador reel, 55
annual award, 4, 10, 95, 96, 123
application (app), 13, 28, 36, 45, 46, 81, 106, 134
Arizona, 141
Atlantic croaker, 22
Atlantic cutlassfish, 96
Atlantic sharpnose shark, 58, 73
Atlantic stingray, 59

BAA, 81, 141
bait ball, 5, 7, 55, 90
barbels, 41
Bass Pro, 5, 88
Berkley line, 5, 88, 171
big fish award, 4, 8, 16, 26, 61-64, 92, 103, 108, 109, 115, 120, 121, 132, 135, 140, 152, 155-158
big game line, 5, 100, 171
billfish, 1, 34, 57
binomial nomenclature system, 24

black buffalo, 59
black crappie, 22, 41, 138, 153
blackfin tuna, 31, 64, 100
blacktip shark, 7, 59, 69, 70, 120
blue catfish, 41, 60, 61, 74, 115-117
blue marlin, 84, 130
blue runner, 17
blue tilapia, 29, 59, 130, 132
bluegill, 12, 13, 38, 84, 99, 112, 113, 134, 147
bluntnose stingray, 59
bonnethead, 58
bottlenose dolphin, 24
bowfishing, 56, 61, 72, 79-82, 115
Bowfishing Association of America (BAA), 81, 141
bragging rights, 67, 69, 70, 74, 87, 103
braided line, 83, 167
Browning fly rod, 46, 123

California, 104
camera, 8, 9, 16, 38-45, 48, 50, 56, 64, 135
cane pole, 83-86, 88

catch and release, 8, 10, 20, 36,
    37, 41, 52, 54, 56, 57, 60, 61,
    63-66, 92, 93, 96, 105, 108,
    113, 121-123, 132, 135, 136
CCA, 101
certificates, 64, 66, 67, 70, 81, 82,
    97, 103, 106, 113, 144
certified scale, 8, 16, 28, 30, 63,
    64, 66, 72,138, 152
channel catfish, 15, 41, 74, 112,
    113, 140, 143, 147
Chatillon scale, 27
chum, 71, 73, 108, 111
Coastal Conservation Association
    (CCA), 101
cobia, 12, 57, 58, 71, 74, 120, 161
Colorado, 105, 165
common carp, 12, 15, 39, 41, 46,
    53, 59, 65, 79, 93, 98, 121,
    140, 141, 143, 150, 162
common snook, 110
Costa Del Mar sunglasses, 105
crevalle jack, 5-8, 58, 70, 79
curve length, 36
cutthroat trout, 95, 96

deckhand, 22, 100, 101, 111, 136,
    138, 155, 156, 158, 161
Destin, Florida, 97, 101
doctorfish, 141
dolphin, 24, 25, 31, 43, 74, 108
Dolphin Docks, Port Aransas,
    Texas, 26, 85, 137, 158
dorado, 24, 25

earthworm, 83, 112, 132, 149
elite angler award, 4, 8, 10, 16, 24,
    26, 39, 40, 61, 62, 85, 108,
    109, 115, 116, 121, 132, 135,
    140, 152, 155, 158

falsifying catch information, 154
FFHF, 8, 13, 31, 36, 48-50, 52,
    54, 55, 63, 64, 72, 77, 85, 90,
    92, 93, 112, 134, 135, 138,
    140, 141
first fish award, 66, 97, 149
fish and wildlife department, 8,
    12, 24, 26, 28, 31, 48, 50,
    66, 73, 78, 81, 83, 112, 121,
    123
fish identification, 21, 22, 24
Fish Nomenclature, 24, 173
Fishes of the Gulf of Mexico, 21
fishing by hand, 73, 74
fitness programs, 105-108
flathead catfish, 74
Florida, 10-12, 22, 25, 31, 38, 43,
    97, 100, 164
Florida Keys, 10, 31, 38, 164
fly fishing, 12, 15, 52, 54, 56, 61,
    63, 72, 73, 84, 86, 90-94,
    103, 113, 115, 118, 122, 123,
    140, 152, 162
fork length, 34, 36
Fort Worth, Texas, 133
Fox Sports Outdoors Report, 105
Fresh Water Fishing Hall of Fame
    (FFHF), 8, 52, 54
freshwater drum, 59, 132
freshwater-fishing.org, 13, 54, 55

gafftopsail catfish, 26, 58
Garcia reel, 5, 55, 108
girth, 6, 36
gizzard shad, 116, 127
goldfish, 141
goliath grouper, 79
grand slam, 108, 110
gray snapper, 31, 74
gray triggerfish, 58, 74-76, 118

INDEX | 181

great barracuda, 17, 31, 43, 44, 79
greater amberjack, 22, 97, 100
green sunfish, 66
guides, 4, 45, 49, 61, 62, 74, 86, 88, 115-117, 134-136, 138-140, 143, 144
Gulf of Mexico, 7, 42, 92
gulf toadfish, 2, 59, 82, 141

hairy blenny, 141
handline fishing, 57, 61, 73, 82, 83, 86, 111, 112, 137
hardhead catfish, 26, 58
hatchery, 13, 134
Hawaii, 24, 130
Hawaiian sling, 78
hybrid striped bass, 18, 59, 62, 63, 134-136, 140
hybrid tilapia, 59, 142

IGFA, 2, 6, 8, 13, 20, 28, 30, 31, 36-38, 45, 48, 50-55, 63, 64, 66, 72, 88, 92, 97, 102, 110, 112, 115, 134, 135, 138, 141, 146, 154
IGFA measuring device, 36, 37
igfa.org, 13, 36, 55
inshore lizardfish, 68
International Game Fish Association (IGFA), 2, 6
internet, 8, 20, 22, 39, 45, 74, 108
invasive species, 166
Islamorada, Florida, 10, 11, 25, 43

juglines, 75, 77
junior angler, 13, 56, 67, 96-98, 115, 149, 164

Kenner boat, 67, 102
king mackerel, 55, 56, 58, 61, 74, 91, 96, 97, 137, 155-159

ladyfish, 26, 58, 63
Lake Granbury, Texas, 98
Lake Lewisville, Texas, 60, 61, 115
Lake Tawakoni, Texas, 115, 135
largemouth bass, 12, 37, 59, 101-103, 105, 112, 113, 119, 127, 130, 134, 143-145, 147, 162
legal-for-trade scale, 8, 16, 28
line class world record, 6
lingcod, 104
lionfish, 141
little tunny, 7, 8, 57, 58, 90, 92, 120
longear sunfish, 13
Louisiana, 10
Lower Laguna Madre, Texas, 78

Magibraid line, 82, 88
mahi-mahi, 24, 25
master angler, 10, 110
measuring board, 16, 32-36, 56, 61, 62, 64, 112, 117, 135, 152, 156
measuring device, 8, 9, 32-34, 36-38, 40, 138
Mirrolure, 5
monofilament, 70, 79, 83, 88, 167, 171
multiple rods, 143, 144
multi-species award, 47, 108, 110, 115, 121, 132, 135, 140, 166
Mustad hook, 16, 51, 82, 100, 111, 112, 121, 127, 143
mutton snapper, 31

nets, 15, 46, 51, 52, 63, 68, 74, 75, 95, 117, 124, 127-129, 132, 141, 143, 144, 151, 162

New York, 140
Nile tilapia, 141
noodling, 74
notary, 21
nurse shark, 32, 33

Oklahoma, 83, 147
open category, 111-113, 115
organizations, 13, 20, 21, 24, 28, 31, 32, 36, 46, 48, 52, 66, 67, 72, 81, 102, 103, 105, 106, 110, 141, 154, 162, 166
Osborn Overkill Knot, 167-171
oscars, 141
other methods category, 20, 57, 62, 73-75, 82, 84-86, 97, 119, 144, 162

pacu, 141
PALA+, 106
paperwork, 9, 18-21, 82, 97
parachute cord, 83, 86, 89
party boats, 22, 97, 101, 104, 111, 136, 137, 155
pearly razorfish, 141
Penn International Reel, 32, 96, 100, 149
photograph, 30, 38-43, 102, 105, 138, 149
pinfish, 58, 82
Plnor, 49, 57, 59, 62, 73, 85-90, 119, 133, 136, 143, 145, 155, 162
pole and line no reel, 54, 57, 62, 83-86, 92, 136, 143, 162
porcupinefish, 157
Port Aransas, Texas, 24, 26, 85, 137, 158
PowerPro braid line, 171
President's Challenge, 106, 107

President's Council on Fitness, Sports, and Nutrition, 106
Presidential Active Lifestyle Award, 106
Presidential Champions Platinum Award, 106
private charters, 136
ProSpec line, 171
protect and conserve the resource, 4, 164, 166

qualification list, 135
quick measurement, 6, 32, 92

rainbow trout, 59, 91, 105, 132, 133
Rapala scale, 27
red drum, 58, 67, 68, 85-88, 108, 130, 134, 136
red grouper, 31
red snapper, 58, 71-75, 97, 100, 105, 108, 111, 120, 122, 126, 136, 155, 161
Reel Deal Lake Whitney Striper Guide, Texas, 49
regulations, 4, 13, 18, 36, 38, 46, 51, 71, 72, 74-78, 82, 83, 92, 102, 119, 123, 144, 150, 166
remora, 57, 58, 73, 74
royal slam, 110
rules, 4, 7, 13, 31, 36, 39, 45, 50-53, 55, 56, 64, 71, 72, 75, 92, 102, 121, 123, 128, 138, 139, 150, 154, 162

safety, 73, 96, 126
sailfish, 19, 38, 39
San Diego, California, 104
sand perch, 57
sand seatrout, 26, 58

sand tilefish, 141
scaled sardines, 155, 156, 158
scales, 6, 8-10, 16, 24, 26-31, 40, 62-64, 66, 72, 112, 113, 124, 135, 138, 152
scientific name, 24
scrawled filefish, 141
Sea Pro boat, 7, 90
setlines, 75, 77, 78
sharksucker, 59, 61, 111, 112, 137
sheepshead, 26, 35
shortfin mako, 149
shrimp, 26, 90, 96, 141, 149
smallmouth bass, 59, 143-145
smallmouth buffalo, 16, 18, 41, 51, 79-81
smartphone, 43, 45, 106
smooth puffer, 21
southern flounder, 26, 78, 79, 102, 108, 110
southern stingray, 78
Spanish mackerel, 5, 7, 8, 43, 55, 56, 58, 70, 85, 90, 120
spearfishing, 78, 79
spinner shark, 7, 59, 70
spotted seatrout, 26, 58, 67, 102, 103, 108, 134
Squaw Creek Reservoir, Texas, 65
squid, 21, 22, 43, 73, 74, 82, 108, 111, 112, 149
striped anchovies, 7
striped bass, 18, 59, 123, 124, 126-128, 134, 135
striped mullet, 63, 102
submittal form, 8, 18, 20, 30, 48, 50, 72
suckermouth catfish, 141

Table 1 - Osborn, Texas State Records, 57-59

tarpon, 10, 11, 31, 32
tenkara, 83-85, 88
Texas, 1, 6, 7, 29, 49, 56, 61, 62, 67, 79, 87, 91-93, 103, 108, 109, 114, 118, 122, 135, 136, 140, 145, 152, 155, 161, 162
Texas Parks and Wildlife Department, 8, 13, 18, 39, 57, 58, 82, 113, 115, 121, 144
threadfin shad, 116, 123
tiger shark, 57
tippet, 20, 51, 52, 54, 71, 72, 92
tip-ups, 77
total length, 34, 36, 135, 136, 152, 158
tournaments, 52, 67, 97, 101, 102, 105, 130, 154, 162, 166
Trinity River, Texas, 75, 133
trophy, 46, 66, 67, 70, 103, 110, 115, 117, 119
trotlines, 74, 75, 77, 81

unconventional methods, 1, 56, 71-73, 75-78, 81, 82
unique species, 140-142
unrestricted categories, 29, 79, 84-86, 97, 112, 144
urban fishing, 132-134
Utah, 78

vacant category, 18, 21, 78, 79, 81, 82, 92, 94, 111-115, 121, 132, 135, 143
vermilion snapper, 31, 58, 71, 97, 100, 111, 137
video, 38-40, 48, 50, 102, 149

wahoo, 101
walleye, 134
waterbody record, 12, 13, 16, 18,

20, 21, 23, 26, 35, 37, 46, 60-
    62, 65, 82, 96, 97, 112, 113,
    121, 124, 132, 135, 136, 141,
    142, 152, 153
webpage or website, 13, 20, 22,
    24, 40, 50, 55-58, 92, 94,
    101, 106, 138, 161
whale shark, 41, 42
white bass, 18, 62, 123, 124, 126-
    128, 134-136
white crappie, 22, 23, 41, 138,
    147, 151, 152
white croaker, 22
white grunt, 22
white snapper, 22
whiterock bass, 62, 135
witnesses, 8, 18, 21, 31, 40, 46-50,
    66, 102

x-rayed, 154

yellow bass, 18
yellowfin tuna, 64, 111, 130
Yellowstone Lake, Wyoming, 95
Yellowstone National Park,
    Wyoming, 95
Yo-Zuri lure, 43

Zebco reel, 66, 79, 82, 147
zeroed, 16, 29, 30

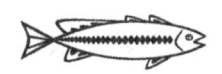

Made in the USA
Monee, IL
10 February 2024